STAR WARS: A NEW HOPE

STAR WARS
A New Hope

George Lucas

faber and faber
LONDON · BOSTON

Published in 1997
by Faber and Faber Limited
3 Queen Square London WC1N 3AU

Photoset by Parker Typesetting Service, Leicester
Printed in England by Mackays of Chatham PLC,
Chatham, Kent

George Lucas is hereby identified as author of this
work in accordance with Section 77 of the Copyright,
Designs and Patents Act 1988

A CIP record for this book
is available from the British Library
ISBN 0-571-19321-8

2 4 6 8 10 9 7 5 3 1

CONTENTS

INTRODUCTION

*The following article was written by Stephen Zito as the young director/
producer, George Lucas, reached a major turning point in his career: on
the eve of the completion of* Star Wars. *Prior to any press screenings.
Prior to the publicity circus. Prior to the signing of the first
merchandising contract. At a time when, to an outsider at least,* Star
Wars *was just another film, not the biggest cinema sensation of all time.*

George Lucas is a contradictory man. Short and slight, he has the
presence of a bigger man. Young by Hollywood standards at
thirty-two, he is the kind of guy you just might entrust with $8
million of your stockholders' money to make a science fiction
movie. In a very public business, he is a private person. He is,
quite simply, a man who wants to have everything his way.

Lucas claims to be shy of the press but he is a good talker. Yet,
he tells you nothing by accident, doesn't let you into his life.

He is one of the most successful of a new breed of Hollywood
film-makers – the bright young man out of film school who jumps
into the industry without the seasoning once required of directors.
Others of his generation include Francis Ford Coppola, John
Milius and Steven Spielberg.

Movies are clearly far more than a means of livelihood; they are
his life. He is, first and foremost, a *film-maker* who got into the
Hollywood studio system by becoming Francis Ford Coppola's
assistant on *The Rain People*. Coppola taught him a lot about
writing and acting, produced Lucas's first film, *THX 1138*, and
lent his name so that Lucas could obtain financing for *American
Graffiti*. *THX 1138*, the expansion of a college-made film, was a
modest critical success, a box-office failure, and something of a
cult favourite. *American Graffiti*, well received by the critics,
became one of the largest moneymakers in the history of film.

What happens when you direct one of the all-time box-office
smashes? Well, everything. You can write your own deal, do what
you want, spend what you please, get your own way. Even up old
scores. What a director does with this freedom tells a lot about the

man. Some sink into self-indulgence, others into conspicuous consumption of movie budgets. George Lucas has used the success of *American Graffiti* to make an $8 million animated comic strip called *Star Wars*.

One cynic, in advance of its completion, has called it *American Graffiti* in outer space. The story, as reconstructed from the Lucas script and the sci-fi novel which bears his name, concerns the adventures of Luke Skywalker, a bored young man who lives with his aunt and uncle on a remote farm on the desert planet of Tatooine, somewhere in the universe. Luke's narrow, confined life is shattered by a message from a kidnapped rebel princess that sets him off on a series of adventures. He soon falls in with a bizarre collection of companions – an old wizard, two robots, a daredevil space freighter pilot and a giant Wookiee.

If this sounds like the stuff of Marvel comics 'sword and sorcery' plots, well, it is just that. (Marvel will even release the story in six instalments this spring.) There is a lot here to charm the pre-adolescent mind – rebellion, interplanetary wars, doomsday machines, space pirates, black knights, magic and sorcery, death stars, mystical happenings, sophisticated torture devices, medieval weaponry and a savage air battle above the grey surface of a killer satellite.

George Lucas does nothing to disguise the fact that *Star Wars* is for the schoolboy in us all. 'I decided I wanted to make a children's movie, to go the Disney route,' Lucas explains in his distinctively nervous manner. 'Fox hates for me to say this, but *Star Wars* has always been intended as a young people's movie. While I set the audience for *Graffiti* at sixteen to eighteen, I set this one at fourteen and maybe even younger than that.'

George Lucas, who wrote the screenplay for and directed this story, found his inspiration among the debris of American popular culture. He *believes*, truly believes, in his boy's own adventure plot, and approaches the pulpish narrative with a sense of wonder and with naive enthusiasm. His original impetus came from the work of Alex Raymond.

'I loved the *Flash Gordon* comic books,' Lucas confesses between bites of his hamburger. 'I loved the Universal serials with Buster Crabbe. After *THX 1138* I wanted to do *Flash Gordon* and tried to buy the rights to it from King Features, but they wanted a lot of money for it, more than I could afford then. They didn't really want to part with the rights – they wanted Fellini to do *Flash Gordon*.

'I realized that *I* could make up a character as easily as Alex Raymond, who took his character from Edgar Rice Burroughs. It's your basic superhero in outer space. I realized that what I really wanted to do was a contemporary action fantasy.'

George Lucas, an avid reader and collector of science fiction literature and art (including a number of Alex Raymond originals), has been greatly influenced by other adventure and fantasy science fiction writers as well. 'As a kid, I read a *lot* of science fiction,' Lucas recalls. 'But instead of reading technical, hard-science writers like Isaac Asimov, I was interested in Harry Harrison and a fantastic, surreal approach to the genre. I grew up on it. *Star Wars* is a sort of compilation of this stuff, but it's never been put in one story before, never put down on film. There is a lot taken from Westerns, mythology and samurai movies. It's all the things that are great put together. It's not like one kind of ice cream but rather a very big sundae.'

Such recent science fiction movies as *Silent Running, Marooned*, or even *2001: A Space Odyssey*, are heavily science-oriented, constructed in accordance with what we know or can formulate about current hardware and technology. The characters are boxed in by probability, logic and common sense. Not so *Star Wars*. The story is set in an alien galaxy with neither temporal nor spatial proximity to our solar system. It takes place in a land of fantasy. This is not *our* future realized: Lucas severs all ties with our solar system.

Lucas also cuts himself off from science. 'It's very surreal and bizarre and has nothing to do with science,' he says of what he mockingly refers to as the film's subtext. 'I wanted it to be an adventure in space, like *John Carter of Mars*. That was before *science* fiction took over, and everything got very serious and science-oriented.

'*Star Wars* has more to do with disclaiming science than anything else. There are very elaborate, Rube Goldberg explanations for things. It's a totally different galaxy with a totally different way of thinking. It's not based on science, which bogs you down. I don't want the movie to be about anything that would happen or be real. I wanted to tell a fantasy story.'

When Lucas and I talked about *Star Wars*, there was no way to judge how successful Lucas had been in making this new movie – which comes out sounding like *American Graffiti* meets *THX*. Not only does Lucas have control over the final cut of the movie, he controls merchandising and publicity as well. Only a handful of the people working on the film, and a couple of key studio executives, had seen the almost-finished film. Part of this secrecy is designed to protect the innovative special effects work, but it is also the result of George Lucas's intense need to control and to personally oversee every aspect of his movie. He is the total film-maker, a self-styled auteur obsessed with hot rods, disaffected adolescents and the glitter of low culture.

If Lucas's labours over the past four years result in a marvellous children's adventure to stand beside movies like *Forbidden Planet* and *This Island Earth*, it will not have been easy. As we finished our lunch, Lucas tells me that he is suffering from bouts of exhaustion, depression and disgust. 'I didn't realize it was going to take so long or be so big or take so much of my life,' he says with the manner of someone on whom fate has played a dirty trick.

All of the four years of *Star Wars* have been difficult for Lucas. This has been his first experience of working on a big-budget picture with a large cast and crew, in which the director must be more than a film-maker. He must be a diplomat, field marshal and nursemaid as well. Perhaps the biggest problem for Lucas has been that, despite the high budget, there has never been quite enough money. 'Although it costs a lot of money,' Lucas says of *Star Wars*, 'it's still a low-budgeted picture. So it's on the same intensity level as a Roger Corman movie only a hundred times bigger. We *still* don't have the luxury of a big movie – time, doing things right. Everything is compromise, cutting corners, not doing this or that. You suffer. You say, "I can't do this," or "That looks terrible, but we'll go with it," which you are normally doing on a $700,000 picture where you're saying, "Get it done!" We're doing that, only it's taking four years. The hard part is, once we started production – which will be two years in May – it's been almost relentless, seven days a week, sixteen hours a day. That's all right for a couple of months, but when it goes on for over a year, it really gets to be a drag.'

Lucas candidly admits that his problems on *Star Wars* were the result of his chronic inability and unwillingness to delegate authority and responsibility. He wants to do it all himself – write, direct, produce, supervise, edit, shoot. He has a hard time letting go. 'I come up from the film-makers' school of doing movies, which means I do everything myself,' Lucas explains. 'If you are a writer director, you *must* get involved with everything. It's very hard for me to get into another system where everybody does things for me, and I say, "Fine." If I ever continue to do these kinds of movies, I've got to learn to do that. I have a lot of friends who can, and I admire them. Francis [Coppola] is going through that now, and he's finally learning, finally getting to the point where he realizes *he* can't do it all. He's getting into the traditional system: "Call me when it's ready, and it better be right, and if it's not, do it again and spend whatever it costs to get it right." But you have to be willing to make *very* expensive movies that way. You can't make cheap movies.

'If I left anything for a day, it would fall apart, and it's purely because I set it up that way and there is nothing I can do about it. It wasn't set up so I could walk away from it. Whenever there is a leak in the dam, I have to stick *my* finger in it. I should learn to say, "Somebody else go plug that up." '

The principal photography on *Star Wars* was completed last summer on location in Tunisia and on forty-five sets spread over eleven sound stages in England. The intervening months have been spent in editing the 340,000 feet of live-action footage and marrying it with the special effects shots being created for Lucas at the two storey warehouse in Van Nuys, which serves as the headquarters for Industrial Light and Magic, an organization of technicians specifically formed to supply *Star Wars* with special effects. The effects work for *Star Wars* has been expensive and painstakingly difficult. Most of the work was done by young and relatively inexperienced effects people rather than by such acknowledged masters of the art as Linwood Dunn and Douglas Trumbull. The reason for this choice of staff was characteristically pragmatic on Lucas's part. With his young staff, he has more control over the special effects than if he had employed an established special effects director with a style, approach and hardware all his own.

'If you hire Trumbull to do your special effects,' Lucas explains, '*he* does your special effects. I was very nervous about that. I wanted to be able to say, "It must look like this, not that." I don't want to be handed an effect at the end of five months and be told, "Here's your special effect, sir." I want to be able to have more say about what's going on. It's really become binary – either you do it yourself, or you don't get a say.

'Technically, you always compare things against *2001*. If you took one of our shots and ran it on the light box and set it next to one of Kubrick's shots, you would say, "Well, his are better." But there is no way, given the time and money we've had, that Kubrick could do any better. He was striving for perfection and had a shot ratio thirty times what we have. When you spend that kind of time and money you can get things perfect. We went into this trying to make a cheap, children's movie for $8 million. We didn't go in and say that we were going to make the perfect science fiction film, but we are gonna make the most spectacular thing you've ever seen!'

The 'we' to which George Lucas occasionally refers includes Gary Kurtz, the producer of *Star Wars* and, like others on the movie, an old and trusted friend of Lucas's. When Lucas talks, Kurtz listens. Only after Lucas returns to San Anselmo do Kurtz and I have the opportunity to talk. He explains that he and Lucas work together with a tense kind of harmony.

'It's a casual arrangement. If you want to categorize the function of the *working* producer, it is to provide all the tools so the director can do everything he wants, or, at least, everything within the limits you are trying to work. I also function as a sounding board to discuss everything that comes up. *Star Wars* is more formally arranged than *Graffiti* was. We made *Graffiti* with eighteen people, but by the time *Star Wars* is finished we will have employed nine hundred people. The larger the picture, the less time you have to deal with detail. On a small picture, you can do everything yourself.'

The burden of coping with production problems in England and Tunisia fell largely to Kurtz. He was responsible in large part for the selection of the British crew: Gil Taylor, the cinematographer who shot *Dr. Strangelove*, *A Hard Day's Night* and *Frenzy*; John Barry, the production designer from *A Clockwork*

Orange; and John Spears, who was in charge of production effects and explosives.

George Lucas is, in many ways, most comfortable with what is known and familiar. He is marvellously adept at the manipulation of the styles and artefacts of the cultural past. Lucas and Kurtz function in many ways like a couple of pack rats. *Star Wars* is literally constructed from bits and pieces of the usable past. During postproduction, model makers at Industrial Light and Magic were busy cannibalizing model kits in order to make spaceships. They used fragments of Kenworth Tractors, Kandy-Vans, Panzer Kampfwagens and even Ford Galaxy 500 XLs to make their spaceships.

This wholesale recycling of the artefacts of the past is nowhere more apparent than in the final gigantic space battle that will take up the last twenty minutes of the movie. The scene is composed of a number of scenes right out of vintage World War II movies. Literally.

'Before the storyboards were done,' Kurtz explains, 'we recorded on videotape any war movie involving aircraft that came up on television, so we had this massive library of parts of old war movies – *The Dam Busters*, *Tora! Tora! Tora!*, *The Battle of Britain*, *Jet Pilot*, *The Bridges at Toko-Ri*, *633 Squadron* and about forty-five other movies. We went through them all and picked out scenes to transfer to film to use as guidelines in the battle.

'We cut them all together into a battle sequence to get an idea of the movement. It was a very bizarre-looking film, all black-and-white, a dirty 16mm dupe. There would be a shot of the pilot saying something, then you cut back to a long shot of the plane, explosions, crashes. It gave a reasonably accurate idea of what the battle sequence would look like, the feeling of it.'

Lucas and Kurtz showed the battle sequences to the special effects people and to the artists who transferred the ersatz movie to storyboards. 'It's very easy to take your hand and fly,' Kurtz says, making an imaginary loop the loop, 'but it's very hard to convert that movement to what John Dykstra and the other special effects people had to do with the models.'

The system that generated the special effects was created by John Dykstra, who received his training under Douglas Trumbull on *The Andromeda Strain* and *Silent Running*. Dykstra, who is the head of Industrial Light and Magic, oversaw the construction of a special computer-run system for making the more than 350 special effects in the film. The key to Dykstra's operation stands in a back room of the warehouse: a giant camera mounted on tracks and powered by high-torque motors under the command of a computer. Each shot is programmed in a computer and played back a number of times to accommodate the various model elements in the shots. The complex special effects system allows Dykstra to create special effects shots with models which approximate the effect of live-action shots.

Dykstra and Lucas didn't always see eye to eye. One of their biggest problems was communication. In special effects, there is always a gap between intention and execution, between conception and realization. Lucas sometimes became angry when the matted shots did not have the authenticity and pace he wanted for the movies. 'Directors and special effects directors always disagree incredibly,' Dykstra says, 'because he conceptualizes one thing but *I* know what is capable of being produced. The major problem we encountered on this show was being able to apply what George started out with conceptually. From the day we met, we talked about World War II dogfight footage which involved lots of action, continuous motion, moving camera, streak, loops and rolls, and all of the things aerial photography allows you to do in live action. This has been difficult to do in special effects with multiple ships, planet backgrounds and stars, because of the problems of angular displacement, matching shots and depth of field.

'It's hard to explain that a concept won't work because of some technological thing, and this becomes a bone of contention. When a director shoots an exterior, he can see the lighting and the set-up and the action and hear the dialogue, but when he comes in here, all there is is a camera running down a track about three inches a second photographing a model. So you have to be able to determine a spatial relationship without having to see the relationship in front of you or being able to compress in your mind's eye five minutes of motion into five seconds. It's more akin to animation than anything else.

'George has to trust me to be able to interpret the drawings and the black-and-white war footage, and that's really hard to do. I don't know if *I* could do that with somebody. That's one of the biggest problems there is.'

Despite their differences of opinion, Dykstra respects Lucas for his single-mindedness, his obsession with getting things right, his love for every frame of *Star Wars*.

'The neat thing about George is that he has a sensibility. He is really involved in his movie, he is really attached. He's hard-headed about stuff, but, if he's wrong, he'll change his mind rather than say, "I'm the director, I've made a decision and that's it." He's got taste. He's got that gift for popular narrative. People like what he does: it's active; it's fast; there's humour in it. *Star Wars* is gonna be exciting all the way. The aerial battle that takes up the last reel of the film is going to be as exciting as the car chase in *The French Connection*.'

During our lunch I had asked Lucas what he wanted from the movie.

'Rather than do some angry, socially relevant film,' he answered, 'I realized there was another relevance that is even more important – dreams and fantasies, getting children to believe there is more to life than garbage and killing and all that real stuff like stealing hubcaps – that you could still sit and dream about exotic lands and strange creatures. Once I got into *Star Wars*, it struck me that we had lost all that – a whole generation was growing up without fairy-tales. You just don't get them any more, and that's the best stuff in the world – adventures in far-off lands. It's *fun*.

'I wanted to do a modern fairy-tale, a myth. One of the criteria of the mythical fairy-tale situation is an exotic, faraway land, but we've lost all the fairy-tale lands on this planet. Every one has disappeared. We no longer have the Mysterious East or treasure islands or going on strange adventures.

'But there is a bigger, mysterious world in space that is more interesting than anything around here. We've just begun to take the first step and can say, "Look! It goes on for a zillion miles out there." You can go anywhere and land on any planet.'

There can be little doubt that George Lucas has gone out on a limb. He has used the success of *American Graffiti* to put on film the dreams and fantasies of his childhood. He has spent $8 million in a genre where movies are usually done as cheaply as possible, resulting in shoddiness. The only question left about *Star Wars* is an old one, frequently asked since the Wright Brothers took their contraption to Kitty Hawk: 'But will it fly?'

(This article excerpted here, first appeared in *American Film*, edited by Hollis Alpert, in April 1977. © American Film Institute.)

STAR WARS
A New Hope

STAR WARS: *A New Hope* was released in the United Kingdom in 1977. The cast and crew includes:

LUKE SKYWALKER	Mark Hamill
HAN SOLO	Harrison Ford
PRINCESS LEIA ORGANA	Carrie Fisher
GRAND MOFF TARKIN	Peter Cushing
SEE-THREEPIO	Anthony Daniels
BEN [OBI-WAN] KENOBI	Alec Guinness
LORD DARTH VADER	David Prowse
VADER'S VOICE	James Earl Jones
CHEWBACCA	Peter Mayhew
ARTOO-DETOO	Kenny Baker

Director	George Lucas
Producer	Gary Kurtz
Screenplay	George Lucas
Photography	Gilbert Taylor, Panavision
Special Photographic Effects	John Dykstra, Industrial Light and Magic
Production Designer	John Barry
Music	John Williams
Editors	Paul Hirsch, Marcia Lucas and Richard Chew

A long time ago in a galaxy far, far away . . .

A vast sea of stars serves as the backdrop for the main title. War drums echo through the heavens as a roll-up slowly crawls into infinity.

It is a period of civil war. Rebel spaceships, striking from a hidden base, have won their first victory against the evil Galactic Empire.

During the battle, Rebel spies managed to steal secret plans to the Empire's ultimate weapon, the Death Star, an armored space station with enough power to destroy an entire planet.

Pursued by the Empire's sinister agents, Princess Leia races home aboard her starship, custodian of the stolen plans that can save her people and restore freedom to the galaxy . . .

The awesome yellow planet of Tatooine emerges from a total eclipse, her two moons glowing against the darkness. A tiny silver spacecraft, a Rebel Blockade Runner firing lasers from the back of the ship, races through space. It is pursued by a giant Imperial starship. Hundreds of deadly laserbolts streak from the Imperial Star Destroyer, causing the main solar fin of the Rebel craft to disintegrate.

INT. REBEL BLOCKADE RUNNER — MAIN PASSAGEWAY

An explosion rocks the ship as two robots, Artoo-Detoo (R2-D2) and See-Threepio (C-3PO), struggle to make their way through the shaking, bouncing passageway. Both robots are old and battered. Artoo is a short, claw-armed tripod. His face is a mass of computer lights surrounding a radar eye. Threepio, on the other hand, is a tall, slender robot of human proportions. He has a gleaming bronze-like metallic surface of an Art Deco design.

Another blast shakes them as they struggle along their way.

3

THREEPIO

Did you hear that? They've shut down the main reactor. We'll be destroyed for sure. This is madness!

Rebel troopers rush past the robots and take up positions in the main passageway. They aim their weapons toward the door.

THREEPIO

We're doomed!

The little R2 unit makes a series of electronic sounds that only another robot could understand.

THREEPIO

There'll be no escape for the Princess this time.

Artoo continues making beeping sounds. Tension mounts as loud metallic latches clank and the screams of heavy equipment are heard moving around the outside hull of the ship.

THREEPIO

What's that?

EXT. SPACECRAFT IN SPACE

The Imperial craft has easily overtaken the Rebel Blockade Runner. The smaller Rebel ship is being drawn into the underside dock of the giant Imperial starship.

INT. REBEL BLOCKADE RUNNER

The nervous Rebel troopers aim their weapons. Suddenly a tremendous blast opens up a hole in the main passageway and a score of fearsome armored spacesuited stormtroopers make their way into the smoke-filled corridor.

In a few minutes the entire passageway is ablaze with laserfire. The deadly bolts ricochet in wild random patterns creating huge explosions. Stormtroopers scatter and duck behind storage lockers. Laserbolts hit several Rebel soldiers, who scream and stagger through the smoke, holding shattered arms and faces.

An explosion hits near the robots.

I should have known better than to trust the logic of a half-sized thermocapsulary dehousing assister . . .

Artoo counters with an angry rebuttal as the battle rages around the two hapless robots.

EXT. TATOOINE – DESERT WASTELAND – DAY

A death-white wasteland stretches from horizon to horizon. The tremendous heat of two huge twin suns settles on a lone figure, Luke Skywalker, a farm boy with heroic aspirations who looks much younger than his eighteen years. His shaggy hair and baggy tunic give him the air of a simple but lovable lad with a prize-winning smile.

A light wind whips at him as he adjusts several valves on a large battered moisture vaporator which sticks out of the desert floor much like an oil pipe with valves. He is aided by a beat-up tread-robot with six claw arms. The little robot appears to be barely functioning and moves with jerky motions. A bright sparkle in the morning sky catches Luke's eye and he instinctively grabs a pair of electrobinoculars from his utility belt. He stands transfixed for a few moments studying the heavens, then dashes towards his dented, crudely repaired landspeeder (an auto-like transport that travels a few feet above the ground on a magnetic field). He motions for the tiny robot to follow him.

LUKE

Hurry up! Come with me! What are you waiting for?! Get in gear!

The robot scoots around in a tight circle, stops short, and smoke begins to pour out of every joint. Luke throws his arms up in disgust. Exasperated, the young farm boy jumps into his landspeeder, leaving the smoldering robot to hum madly.

INT. REBEL BLOCKADE RUNNER – MAIN HALLWAY

The awesome, seven-foot-tall Dark Lord of the Sith makes his way into the blinding light of the main passageway. This is Darth Vader, right hand of the Emperor. His face is obscured by his flowing black robes and grotesque breath mask, which stands out next to the fascist white armored suits of the Imperial stormtroopers.

5

*Everyone instinctively backs away from the imposing warrior and a
deathly quiet sweeps through the Rebel troops. Several of the Rebel
troops break and run in a frenzied panic.*

INT. REBEL BLOCKADE RUNNER

*A woman's hand puts a card into an opening in Artoo's dome. Artoo
makes beeping sounds.*

INT. REBEL BLOCKADE RUNNER

*Threepio stands in a hallway, somewhat bewildered. Artoo is nowhere
in sight. The pitiful screams of the doomed Rebel soldiers can be heard in
the distance.*

THREEPIO

Artoo! Artoo-Detoo, where are you?

*A familiar clanking sound attracts Threepio's attention and he spots
little Artoo at the end of the hallway in a smoke-filled alcove. A
beautiful young girl (about sixteen years old) stands in front of Artoo.
Surreal and out of place, dreamlike and half hidden in the smoke, she*

finishes adjusting something on Artoo's computer face, then watches as the little robot joins his companion.

THREEPIO
At last! Where have you been?

Stormtroopers can be heard battling in the distance.

THREEPIO
They're heading in this direction. What are we going to do? We'll be sent to the spice mine of Kessel or smashed into who-knows-what!

Artoo scoots past his bronze friend and races down the subhallway. Threepio chases after him.

THREEPIO
Wait a minute, where are you going?

Artoo responds with electronic beeps.

INT. REBEL BLOCKADE RUNNER – CORRIDOR

The evil Darth Vader stands amid the broken and twisted bodies of his foes. He grabs a wounded Rebel Officer by the neck as an Imperial Officer rushes up to the Dark Lord.

IMPERIAL OFFICER
The Death Star plans are not in the main computer.

Vader squeezes the neck of the Rebel, who struggles in vain.

VADER
Where are those transmissions you intercepted?

Vader lifts the Rebel off his feet by his throat.

REBEL OFFICER
We intercepted no transmissions. Aaah . . . This is a consular ship. We're on a diplomatic mission.

VADER
If this is a consular ship . . . where is the Ambassador?

The Rebel refuses to speak but eventually cries out as the Dark Lord begins to squeeze the officer's throat, creating a gruesome snapping and choking, until the soldier goes limp. Vader tosses the dead soldier against the wall and turns to his troops.

VADER

Commander, tear this ship apart until you've found those plans and bring me the Ambassador. I want her alive!

The stormtroopers scurry into the subhallways.

INT. REBEL BLOCKADE RUNNER – SUBHALLWAY

The lovely young girl huddles in a small alcove as the stormtroopers search through the ship. She is Princess Leia Organa, a member of the Alderaan Senate. The fear in her eyes slowly gives way to anger as the muted crushing sounds of the approaching stormtroopers grow louder. One of the troopers spots her.

TROOPER

There she is! Set for stun!

Leia steps from her hiding place and blasts a trooper with her laser pistol. She starts to run but is felled by a paralyzing ray. The troopers inspect her inert body.

TROOPER

She'll be all right. Inform Lord Vader we have a prisoner.

INT. REBEL BLOCKADE RUNNER – SUBHALLWAY

Artoo stops before the small hatch of an emergency lifepod. He snaps the seal on the main latch and a red warning light begins to flash. The stubby astro-robot works his way into the cramped four-man pod.

THREEPIO

Hey, you're not permitted in there. It's restricted. You'll be deactivated for sure.

Artoo beeps something to him.

THREEPIO

Don't call me a mindless philosopher, you overweight glob of grease! Now come out before somebody sees you.

Artoo whistles something at his reluctant friend regarding the mission he is about to perform.

8

THREEPIO

Secret mission? What plans? What are you talking about? I'm not getting in there!

Artoo isn't happy with Threepio's stubbornness, and he beeps and twangs angrily.

A new explosion, this time very close, sends dust and debris through the narrow subhallway. Flames lick at Threepio and, after a flurry of electronic swearing from Artoo, the lanky robot jumps into the lifepod.

THREEPIO

I'm going to regret this.

INT. REBEL BLOCKADE RUNNER

The safety door snaps shut, and with the thunder of exploding latches the tiny lifepod ejects from the disabled ship.

INT. IMPERIAL STAR DESTROYER

On the main viewscreen, the lifepod carrying the two terrified robots speeds away from the stricken Rebel spacecraft.

CHIEF PILOT

There goes another one.

CAPTAIN

Hold your fire. There are no life forms. It must have been short-circuited.

INT. LIFEPOD

Artoo and Threepio look out at the receding Imperial starship. Stars circle as the pod rotates through the galaxy.

THREEPIO

That's funny, the damage doesn't look as bad from out here.

Artoo beeps an assuring response.

THREEPIO

Are you sure this thing is safe?

EXT. TATOOINE — ANCHORHEAD SETTLEMENT — POWER STATION — DAY

Heat waves radiate from the dozen or so bleached white buildings. Luke pilots his landspeeder through the dusty empty street of the tiny settlement. An old Woman runs to get out of the way of the speeding vehicle, shaking her first at Luke as he flies past.

> WOMAN
> I've told you kids to slow down!

Luke pulls up behind a low concrete service station that is all but covered by the shifting desert sands.

INT. POWER STATION — DAY

Luke bursts into the power station, waking The Fixer, a rugged mechanic, and Camie, a sexy, disheveled girl who has been asleep on his lap. They grumble as he races through the office, yelling wildly.

> FIXER
> Did I hear a young noise blast through here?

> CAMIE
> It was just Wormie on another rampage.

Luke bounces into a small room behind the office where Deak and Windy, two tough boys about the same age as Luke, are playing a computer pool-like game with Biggs, a burly, handsome boy a few years older than the rest. His flashy city attire is a sharp contrast to the loose-fitting tunics of the farm boys. A robot repairs some equipment in the background.

> LUKE
> Shape it up you guys! . . . Biggs?

Luke's surprise at the appearance of Biggs gives way to great joy and emotion. They give each other a great bear hug.

> LUKE
> I didn't know you were back! When did you get in?

> BIGGS
> Just now. I wanted to surprise you, hot shot. I thought you'd be here . . . certainly didn't expect you to be out working.

(laughs)

LUKE

The Academy didn't change you much . . . but you're back so soon? Hey, what happened, didn't you get your commission?

Biggs has an air of cool that seems slightly phony.

BIGGS

Of course I got it. Signed aboard the *Rand Ecliptic* last week. First mate Biggs Darklighter at your service . . .
(he salutes)
. . . I just came back to say goodbye to all you unfortunate landlocked simpletons.

Everyone laughs. The dazzling spectacle of his dashing friend is almost too much for Luke, but suddenly he snaps out of it.

LUKE

I almost forgot. There's a battle going on! Right here in our system. Come and look!

DEAK

Not again! Forget it.

EXT. TATOOINE – ANCHORHEAD SETTLEMENT – POWER STATION – DAY

The group stumbles out into the stifling desert sun. Camie and The fixer complain and are forced to shade their eyes. Luke has his electrobinoculars out scanning the heavens.

LUKE

There they are!

Biggs takes the electrobinoculars from Luke as the others strain to see something with the naked eye. Through the electrobinoculars Biggs sees two small silver specks.

BIGGS

That's no battle, hot shot . . . they're just sitting there! Probably a freighter-tanker refueling.

LUKE

But there was a lot of firing earlier . . .

Camie grabs the electrobinoculars away, banging them against the building in the process. Luke grabs them.

LUKE

Hey, easy with those . . .

CAMIE

Don't worry about it, Wormie.

The Fixer gives Luke a hard look and the young farm boy shrugs his shoulders in resignation.

FIXER

I keep telling you, the Rebellion is a long way from here. I doubt if the Empire would even fight to keep this system. Believe me, Luke, this planet is a big hunk of nothing . . .

Luke agrees, although it's obvious he isn't sure why. The group stumbles back into the power station grumbling about Luke's ineptitude.

INT. REBEL BLOCKADE RUNNER – HALLWAY

Princess Leia is led down a low-ceilinged hallway by a squad of armored stormtroopers. Her hands are bound and she is brutally shoved when she is unable to keep up with the briskly marching troops. They stop in a smoky hallway as Darth Vader emerges from the shadows. The sinister Dark Lord stares hard at the frail young senator, but she doesn't move.

LEIA

Lord Vader. I should have known. Only you could be so bold. The Imperial Senate will not sit still for this, when they hear you've attacked a diplomatic . . .

VADER

Don't play games with me, Your Highness. You weren't on any mercy mission this time. You passed directly through a restricted system. Several transmissions were beamed to this ship by Rebel spies. I want to know what happened to the plans they sent you.

LEIA

I don't know what you're talking about. I'm a member of the Imperial Senate on a diplomatic mission to Alderaan . . .

VADER

You're a part of the Rebel Alliance . . . and a traitor. Take her away!

Leia is marched away down the hallway and into the smoldering hole blasted in the side of the ship. An Imperial Commander turns to Vader.

COMMANDER

Holding her is dangerous. If word of this gets out, it could generate sympathy for the Rebellion in the senate.

VADER

I have traced the Rebel spies to her. Now she is my only link to find their secret base.

COMMANDER

She'll die before she'll tell you anything.

VADER

Leave that to me. Send a distress signal and then inform the senate that all aboard were killed!

Another Imperial Officer approaches Vader and the commander. They stop and snap to attention.

SECOND OFFICER

Lord Vader, the battle station plans are not aboard this ship! And no transmissions were made. An escape pod was jettisoned during the fighting, but no life forms were aboard.

Vader turns to the commander.

VADER

She must have hidden the plans in the escape pod. Send a detachment down to retrieve them. See to it personally, Commander. There'll be no one to stop us this time.

SECOND OFFICER

Yes, sir.

EXT. SPACE

The Imperial Star Destroyer comes over the surface of the planet Tatooine.

Jundland, or 'No Man's Land,' where the rugged desert mesas meet the foreboding dune sea. The two helpless astro-robots kick up clouds of sand as they leave the lifepod and clumsily work their way across the desert wasteland. The lifepod in the distance rests half-buried in the sand.

THREEPIO

How did we get into this mess? I really don't know how. We seem to be made to suffer. It's our lot in life.

Artoo answers with beeping sounds.

THREEPIO

I've got to rest before I fall apart. My joints are almost frozen.

Artoo continues to respond with beeping sounds.

THREEPIO

What a desolate place this is.

Suddenly Artoo whistles, makes a sharp right turn and starts off in the direction of the rocky desert mesas. Threepio stops and yells at him.

THREEPIO

Where are you going?

A stream of electronic noises pours forth from the small robot.

THREEPIO

Well, I'm not going that way. It's much too rocky. This way is much easier.

Artoo counters with a long whistle.

THREEPIO

What makes you think there are settlements over there?

Artoo continues to make beeping sounds.

THREEPIO

Don't get technical with me.

Artoo continues to make beeping sounds.

THREEPIO

What mission? What are you talking about? I've had just

about enough of you! Go that way! You'll be malfunctioning within a day, you nearsighted scrap pile!

He gives the little robot a kick and starts on in the direction of the vast dune sea.

THREEPIO

And don't let me catch you following me begging for help, because you won't get it.

Artoo's reply is a rather rude sound. He turns and trudges out in the direction of the towering mesas.

THREEPIO

No more adventures. I'm not going that way.

Artoo beeps to himself as he makes his way towards the distant mountains.

EXT. TATOOINE – DUNE SEA

Threepio, hot and tired, struggles up over the ridge of a dune: only to find more dunes, which seem to go on for endless miles. He looks back in the direction of the now distant rock mesas.

THREEPIO

That malfunctioning little twerp. This is all his fault! He tricked me into going this way, but he'll do no better.

In a huff of anger and frustration, Threepio knocks the sand from his joints. His plight seems hopeless, when a glint of reflected light in the distance reveals an object moving toward him.

THREEPIO

Wait, what's that? A transport! I'm saved!

The bronze droid waves frantically and yells at the approaching transport.

THREEPIO

Over here! Help! Please, help!

EXT. TATOOINE – ANCHORHEAD SETTLEMENT – POWER STATION – DAY

Luke and Biggs are walking and drinking a malt brew. Fixer and the others can be heard working inside.

LUKE
(*very animated*)
. . . so I cut off my power, shut down the afterburners and came in low on Deak's trail. I was so close I thought I was going to fry my instruments. As it was I busted up the skyhopper pretty bad. Uncle Owen was pretty upset. He grounded me for the rest of the season. You should have been there . . . it was fantastic.

BIGGS
You ought to take it a little easy, Luke. You may be the hottest bushpilot this side of Mos Eisley, but those little skyhoppers are dangerous. Keep it up, and one day, whammo, you're going to be nothing more than a dark spot on the down side of a canyon wall.

LUKE
Look who's talking. Now that you've been around those giant starships you're beginning to sound like my uncle. You've gotten soft in the city . . .

BIGGS
I've missed you, kid.

LUKE
Well, things haven't been the same since you left, Biggs. It's been so . . . quiet.

Biggs looks around then leans close to Luke.

BIGGS
Luke, I didn't come back just to say goodbye . . . I shouldn't tell you this, but you're the only one I can trust . . . and if I don't come back, I want somebody to know.

Luke's eyes are wide with Biggs's seriousness and loyalty.

LUKE
What are you talking about?

BIGGS
I made some friends at the Academy.

17

(*he whispers*)
. . . when our frigate goes to one of the central systems, we're
going to jump ship and join the Alliance . . .

Luke, amazed and stunned, is almost speechless.

LUKE

Join the Rebellion?! Are you kidding! How?

BIGGS

Quiet down, will ya! You got a mouth bigger than a meteor
crater!

LUKE

I'm sorry. I'm quiet.
(*he whispers*)
Listen how quiet I am. You can barely hear me . . .

Biggs shakes his head angrily and then continues.

BIGGS

My friend has a friend on Bestine who might help us make
contact.

LUKE

You're crazy! You could wander around forever trying to find
them.

BIGGS

I know it's a long shot, but if I don't find them I'll do what I
can on my own . . . It's what we always talked about. Luke,
I'm not going to wait for the Empire to draft me into service.
The Rebellion is spreading and I want to be on the right side
— the side I believe in.

LUKE

And I'm stuck here . . .

BIGGS

I thought you were going to the Academy next term. You'll
get your chance to get off this rock.

LUKE

Not likely! I had to cancel my application. There has been a

lot of unrest among the Sand People since you left . . .
they've even raided the outskirts of Anchorhead.

BIGGS

Your uncle could hold off a whole colony of Sand People
with one blaster.

LUKE

I know, but he's got enough vaporators going to make the
place pay off. He needs me for just one more season. I can't
leave him now.

BIGGS

I feel for you, Luke, you're going to have to learn what seems
to be important or what really is important. What good is all
your uncle's work if it's taken over by the Empire? . . . You
know they're starting to nationalize commerce in the central
systems . . . it won't be long before your uncle is merely a
tenant, slaving for the greater glory of the Empire.

LUKE

It couldn't happen here. You said it yourself. The Empire
won't bother with this rock.

BIGGS

Things always change.

LUKE

I wish I was going . . . Are you going to be around long?

BIGGS

No, I'm leaving in the morning . . .

LUKE

Then I guess I won't see you.

BIGGS

Maybe someday . . . I'll keep a lookout.

LUKE

Well, I'll be at the Academy next season . . . after that who
knows. I won't be drafted into the Imperial Starfleet, that's
for sure . . . Take care of yourself, you'll always be the best
friend I've got.

So long, Luke.

Biggs turns away from his old friend and heads back towards the power station.

EXT. TATOOINE – ROCK CANYON – SUNSET

The gargantuan rock formations are shrouded in a strange foreboding mist and the ominous sounds of unearthly creatures fill the air. Artoo moves cautiously through the creepy rock canyon, inadvertently making a loud clicking noise as he goes. He hears a distant, hard, metallic sound and stops for a moment. Convinced he is alone, he continues on his way.

In the distance, a pebble tumbles down the steep canyon wall and a small dark figure darts into the shadows. A little further up the canyon a slight flicker of lights reveals a pair of eyes in the dark recesses only a few feet from the narrow path.

The unsuspecting robot waddles along the rugged trail until suddenly, out of nowhere, a powerful magnetic ray shoots out of the rocks and engulfs him in an eerie glow. He manages one short electronic squeak before he topples over on to his back. His bright computer lights flicker off, then on, then off again. Out of the rocks scurry three Jawas, no taller than Artoo. They holster strange and complex weapons as they cautiously approach the robot. They wear grubby cloaks and their faces are shrouded so that only their glowing yellow eyes can be seen. They hiss and make odd guttural sounds as they heave the heavy robot on to their shoulders and carry him off down the trail.

EXT. TATOOINE – ROCK CANYON – SANDCRAWLER – SUNSET

The eight Jawas carry Artoo out of the canyon to a huge tank-like vehicle the size of a four-story house. They weld a small disk on the side of Artoo and then put him under a large tube on the side of the vehicle and the little robot is sucked into the giant machine.

The filthy little Jawas scurry like rats up small ladders and enter the main cabin of the behemoth transport.

INT. SANDCRAWLER – HOLD AREA

It is dim inside the hold area of the sandcrawler. Artoo switches on a small floodlight on his forehead and stumbles around the scrap heap. The narrow beam swings across rusty metal rocket parts and an array of grotesquely twisted and maimed astro-robots. He lets out a pathetic electronic whimper and stumbles off towards what appears to be a door at the end of the chamber.

INT. SANDCRAWLER – PRISON AREA

Artoo enters a wide room with a four-foot ceiling. In the middle of the scrap heap sit a dozen or so robots of various shapes and sizes. Some are engaged in electronic conversation, while others simply mill about. A voice of recognition calls out from the gloom.

THREEPIO

Artoo-Detoo! It's you! It's you!

A battered Threepio scrambles up to Artoo and embraces him.

EXT. TATOOINE – ROCK CANYON – SANDCRAWLER – SUNSET

The enormous sandcrawler lumbers off towards the magnificent twin suns, which are slowly setting over a distant mountain ridge.

EXT. TATOOINE – DESERT – DAY

Four Imperial stormtroopers mill about in front of the half-buried life-pod that brought Artoo and Threepio to Tatooine. A trooper yells to an officer some distance away.

FIRST TROOPER

Someone was in the pod. The tracks go off in this direction.

A second trooper picks up a small bit of metal out of the sand and gives it to the first trooper.

SECOND TROOPER

Look, sir – droids.

EXT. TATOOINE – DUNES

The sandcrawler moves slowly down a great sand dune.

INT. SANDCRAWLER

Threepio and Artoo noisily bounce along inside the cramped prison chamber. Artoo appears to be shut off.

THREEPIO

Wake up! Wake up!

Suddenly the shaking and bouncing of the sandcrawler stops, creating quite a commotion among the mechanical men. Threepio's fist bangs the head of Artoo whose computer lights pop on as he begins beeping. At the far end of the long chamber a hatch opens, filling the chamber with blinding white light. A dozen or so Jawas make their way through the odd assortment of robots.

THREEPIO

We're doomed.

A Jawa starts moving towards them.

THREEPIO

Do you think they'll melt us down?

Artoo responds, making beeping sounds.

THREEPIO

Don't shoot! Don't shoot! Will this never end?

EXT. TATOOINE – DESERT – LARS HOMESTEAD – AFTERNOON

The Jawas mutter gibberish as they busily line up their battered captives, including Artoo and Threepio, in front of the enormous sandcrawler, which is parked beside a small homestead consisting of three large holes in the ground surrounded by several tall moisture vaporators and one small adobe block house.

The Jawas scurry around fussing over the robots, straightening them up or brushing some dust from a dented metallic elbow. The shrouded little creatures smell horribly, attracting small insects to the dark areas where their mouths and nostrils should be.

Out of the shadows of a dingy side-building limps Owen Lars, a large burly man in his mid-fifties. His reddish eyes are sunken in a dust-covered face. As the farmer carefully inspects each of the robots, he is closely followed by his slump-shouldered nephew, Luke Skywalker. One of the vile little Jawas walks ahead of the farmer spouting an animated sales pitch in a queer, unintelligible language.

A voice calls out from one of the huge holes that form the homestead. Luke goes over to the edge and sees his Aunt Beru standing in the main courtyard.

BERU

Luke, tell Owen that if he gets a translator to be sure it speaks Bocce.

LUKE

It looks like we don't have much of a choice but I'll remind him.

Luke returns to his uncle as they look over the equipment for sale with the Jawa leader.

OWEN

I have no need for a protocol droid.

THREEPIO
(*quickly*)

Sir – not in an environment such as this – that's why I've also been programmed for over thirty secondary functions that . . .

OWEN

What I really need is a droid that understands the binary languages of moisture vaporators.

THREEPIO

Vaporators! Sir – my first job was programming binary load lifters . . . very similar to your vaporators. You could say . . .

OWEN

Do you speak Bocce?

THREEPIO

Of course I can, sir. It's like a second language for me . . . I'm as fluent in Bocce . . .

OWEN

All right; shut up!

(*turning to Jawa*)

I'll take this one.

THREEPIO

Shutting up, sir.

OWEN

Luke, take these two over to the garage, will you? I want you to have both of them cleaned up before dinner.

LUKE

But I was going into Toshi Station to pick up some power converters . . .

OWEN

You can waste time with your friends when your chores are done. Now, come on, get to it!

LUKE

All right, come on! And the red one, come on. Well, come on, Red, let's go.

As the Jawas start to lead the three remaining robots back into the sandcrawler, Artoo lets out a pathetic little beep and starts after his old friend Threepio. He is restrained by a slimy Jawa, who zaps him with a control box.

Owen is negotiating with the head Jawa. Luke and the two robots start for the garage when a plate pops off the head of the red astro-droid, throwing parts all over the ground. He adjusts the astro-droid's head plate and it sparks wildly.

LUKE

Uncle Owen . . .

OWEN

Yeah?

LUKE

This R2 unit has a bad motivator. Look!

OWEN
(*to the head Jawa*)
Hey, what're you trying to push on us?

The Jawa goes into a loud spiel. Meanwhile, Artoo has sneaked out of line and is moving up and down trying to attract attention. He lets out with a low whistle. Threepio taps Luke on the shoulder.

THREEPIO
(*pointing to Artoo*)
Excuse me, sir, but that R2 unit is in prime condition. A real bargain.

LUKE
Uncle Owen . . .

OWEN
Yeah?

LUKE
What about that one?

OWEN
(*to Jawa*)
What about that blue one? We'll take that one.

With a little reluctance the scruffy dwarf trades the damaged astro-robot for Artoo.

LUKE
Yeah, take this away.

THREEPIO
Uh, I'm quite sure you'll be very pleased with that one, sir. He really is in first-class condition. I've worked with him before. Here he comes.

Owen pays off the whining Jawa and the two robots trudge off towards a grimy homestead entry.

LUKE
Okay, let's go.

THREEPIO
(*to Artoo*)
Now, don't forget this! Why I should stick my neck out for you is quite beyond my capacity!

INT. LARS HOMESTEAD — GARAGE AREA — LATE AFTERNOON

The garage is cluttered and worn, but a friendly, peaceful atmosphere permeates the low gray chamber. Threepio lowers himself into a large tub filled with warm oil. Near the battered landspeeder little Artoo rests on a large battery with a cord attached to his face.

THREEPIO
Thank the maker! This oil bath is going to feel so good. I've got such a bad case of dust contamination, I can barely move!

Artoo beeps a muffled reply. Luke seems to be lost in thought as he runs his hand over the damaged fin of a small two-man skyhopper spaceship resting in a low hangar off the garage. Finally Luke's frustrations get the better of him and he slams a wrench across the workbench.

LUKE
It just isn't fair. Oh, Biggs is right. I'm never gonna get out of here!

THREEPIO
Is there anything I might do to help?

Luke glances at the battered robot. A bit of his anger drains and a tiny smile creeps across his face.

LUKE
Well, not unless you can alter time, speed up the harvest, or teleport me off this rock!

THREEPIO
I don't think so, sir. I'm only a droid and not very knowledgeable about such things. Not on this planet, anyway. As a matter of fact, I'm not even sure which planet I'm on.

LUKE
Well, if there's a bright center to the universe, you're on the planet that it's farthest from.

THREEPIO

I see, sir.

LUKE

Uh, you can call me Luke.

THREEPIO

I see, Sir Luke.

LUKE
(*laughing*)

Just Luke.

THREEPIO

And I am See-Threepio, human–cyborg relations, and this is my counterpart, Artoo-Detoo.

LUKE

Hello.

Artoo beeps in response. Luke unplugs Artoo and begins to scrape several connectors on the robot's head with a chrome pick. Threepio climbs out of the oil tub and begins wiping oil from his bronze body.

LUKE

You got a lot of carbon scoring here. It looks like you boys have seen a lot of action.

THREEPIO

With all we've been through, sometimes I'm amazed we're in as good condition as we are, what with the Rebellion and all.

Luke sparks to life at the mention of the Rebellion.

LUKE

You know of the Rebellion against the Empire?

THREEPIO

That's how we came to be in your service, if you take my meaning, sir.

LUKE

Have you been in many battles?

THREEPIO

Several, I think. Actually, there's not much to tell. I'm not much more than an interpreter, and not very good at telling stories. Well, not at making them interesting, anyway.

Luke struggles to remove a small metal fragment from Artoo's neck joint. He uses a larger pick.

LUKE

Well, my little friend, you've got something jammed in here real good. Were you on a starcruiser or . . .

The fragment breaks loose with a snap, sending Luke tumbling head over heels. He sits up and sees a twelve-inch three-dimensional hologram of Leia Organa, the Rebel senator, being projected from the face of little Artoo. The image is a rainbow of colors as it flickers and jiggles in the dimly lit garage. Luke's mouth hangs open in awe.

LEIA

Help me, Obi-Wan Kenobi. You're my only hope.

LUKE

What's this?

Artoo looks around and sheepishly beeps an answer for Threepio to translate.

Leia continues to repeat the sentence fragment over and over.

THREEPIO

What is what?!? He asked you a question . . .
(*pointing at Leia*)
What is that?

Artoo whistles his surprise as he pretends to just notice the hologram. He looks around and sheepishly beeps an answer for Threepio to translate. Leia continues to repeat the sentence fragment over and over.

LEIA

Help me, Obi-Wan Kenobi. You're my only hope.
Help me, Obi-Wan Kenobi. You're my only hope.

THREEPIO

Oh, he says it's nothing, sir. Merely a malfunction. Old data. Pay it no mind.

Luke becomes intrigued by the beautiful young girl.

LUKE

Who is she? She's beautiful.

THREEPIO

I'm afraid I'm not quite sure, sir.

LEIA

Help me, Obi-Wan Kenobi . . .

THREEPIO

I think she was a passenger on our last voyage. A person of some importance, sir — I believe. Our captain was attached to . . .

LUKE

Is there more to this recording?

Luke reaches for Artoo but he lets out several frantic squeaks and a whistle.

THREEPIO

Behave yourself, Artoo. You're going to get us in trouble. It's all right, you can trust him. He's our new master.

Artoo whistles and beeps a long message to Threepio.

THREEPIO

He says he's the property of Obi-Wan Kenobi, a resident of these parts. And it's a private message for him. Quite frankly, sir, I don't know what he's talking about. Our last master was Captain Antilles, but with what we've been through, this little R2 unit has become a bit eccentric.

LUKE

Obi-Wan Kenobi? I wonder if he means old Ben Kenobi?

THREEPIO

I beg your pardon, sir, but do you know what he's talking about?

LUKE

Well, I don't know anyone named Obi-Wan, but old Ben lives out beyond the dune sea. He's kind of a strange old hermit.

Luke gazes at the beautiful young princess for a few moments.

LUKE

I wonder who she is. It sounds like she's in trouble. I'd better play back the whole thing.

Artoo beeps something to Threepio.

THREEPIO

He says the restraining bolt has short-circuited his recording system. He suggests that if you remove the bolt, he might be able to play back the entire recording.

Luke looks longingly at the lovely, little princess and hasn't really heard what Threepio has been saying.

LUKE

Hm? Oh, yeah, well, I guess you're too small to run away on me if I take this off! Okay.

Luke takes a wedged bolt and pops the restraining bolt off Artoo's side.

LUKE

There you go.

The princess immediately disappears.

LUKE

Well, wait a minute. Where'd she go? Bring her back! Play back the entire message.

Artoo beeps an innocent reply as Threepio sits up in embarrassment.

THREEPIO

What message? The one you've just been playing. The one you're carrying inside your rusty innards!

A woman's voice calls out from the other room.

AUNT BERU

Luke? Luke! Come to dinner!

Luke stands up and shakes his head at the malfunctioning robot.

LUKE

All right, I'll be right there, Aunt Beru.

THREEPIO
I'm sorry, sir, but he appears to have picked up a slight flutter.

Luke tosses Artoo's restraining bolt on the workbench and hurries out of the room.

LUKE
Well, see what you can do with him. I'll be right back.

THREEPIO
(*to Artoo*)
Just you reconsider playing that message for him.

Artoo beeps in response.

THREEPIO
No, I don't think he likes you at all.

Artoo beeps.

THREEPIO
No, I don't like you either.

INT. LARS HOMESTEAD – DINING AREA

Luke's Aunt Beru, a warm, motherly woman, fills a pitcher with blue fluid from a refrigerated container in the well-used kitchen. She puts the pitcher on a tray with some bowls of food and starts for the dining area.

Luke sits with his Uncle Owen before a table covered with steaming bowls of food as Aunt Beru carries in a bowl of red grain.

LUKE
You know, I think that R2 unit we bought might have been stolen.

OWEN
What makes you think that?

LUKE
Well, I stumbled across a recording while I was cleaning him. He says he belongs to someone called Obi-Wan Kenobi.

Owen is greatly alarmed at the mention of this name, but manages to control himself.

LUKE

I thought he might have meant old Ben. Do you know what he's talking about? Well, I wonder if he's related to Ben.

Owen breaks loose with a fit of uncontrolled anger.

OWEN

That old man's just a crazy wizard. Tomorrow I want you to take that R2 unit into Anchorhead and have its memory flushed. That'll be the end of it. It belongs to us now.

LUKE

But what if this Obi-Wan comes looking for him?

OWEN

He won't. I don't think he exists any more. He died about the same time as your father.

LUKE

He knew my father?

OWEN

I told you to forget it. Your only concern is to prepare the new droids for tomorrow. In the morning I want them on the south ridge working on those condensers.

LUKE

Yes, sir. I think those new droids are going to work out fine. In fact, I, uh, was also thinking about our agreement about my staying on another season. And if these new droids do work out, I want to transmit my application to the Academy this year.

Owen's face becomes a scowl, although he tries to suppress it.

OWEN

You mean the next semester before harvest?

LUKE

Sure. There's more than enough droids.

OWEN

Harvest is when I need you the most. Only one more season. This year we'll make enough on the harvest so I'll be able to hire some more hands. And then you can go to the Academy next year.

Luke continues to toy with his food, not looking at his uncle.

> OWEN

You must understand I need you here, Luke.

> LUKE

But, it's a whole 'nother year.

> OWEN

Look, it's only one more season.

Luke pushes his half-eaten plate of food aside and stands.

> LUKE

Yeah, that's what you said last year when Biggs and Tank left.

> AUNT BERU

Where are you going?

> LUKE

It looks like I'm going nowhere. I have to finish cleaning those droids.

Resigned to his fate, Luke paddles out of the room. Owen mechanically finishes his dinner.

> AUNT BERU

Owen, he can't stay here for ever. Most of his friends have gone. It means so much to him.

> OWEN

I'll make it up to him next year. I promise.

> AUNT BERU

Luke's just not a farmer, Owen. He has too much of his father in him.

> OWEN

That's what I'm afraid of.

EXT. TATOOINE – LARS HOMESTEAD

The giant twin suns of Tatooine slowly disappear behind a distant dune range. Luke stands watching them for a few moments, then reluctantly enters the domed entrance to the homestead.

33

INT. LARS HOMESTEAD — GARAGE

Luke enters the garage to discover the robots nowhere in sight. He takes a small control box from his utility belt similar to the one the Jawas were carrying. He activates the box, which creates a low hum, and Threepio, letting out a short yell, pops up from behind the skyhopper spaceship.

LUKE
What are you doing hiding there?

Threepio stumbles forward, but Artoo is still nowhere in sight.

THREEPIO
It wasn't my fault, sir. Please don't deactivate me. I told him not to go, but he's faulty, malfunctioning; kept babbling on about his mission.

LUKE
Oh, no!

Luke races out of the garage, followed by Threepio.

EXT. TATOOINE – LARS HOMESTEAD

Luke rushes out of the small domed entry to the homestead and searches the darkening horizon for the small tripod astro-robot. Threepio struggles out of the homestead and on to the salt flat as Luke scans the landscape with his electrobinoculars.

> **THREEPIO**
>
> That R2 unit has always been a problem. These astro-droids are getting quite out of hand. Even I can't understand their logic at times.

> **LUKE**
>
> How could I be so stupid? He's nowhere in sight. Blast it!

> **THREEPIO**
>
> Pardon me, sir, but couldn't we go after him?

> **LUKE**
>
> It's too dangerous with all the Sand People around. We'll have to wait until morning.

> **OWEN**
> *(yelling from the homestead plaza)*
>
> Luke, I'm shutting the power down for the night.

> **LUKE**
>
> All right, I'll be there in a few minutes. Boy, am I gonna get it.

He takes one final look across the dim horizon.

> **LUKE**
>
> You know, that little droid is going to cause me a lot of trouble.

> **THREEPIO**
>
> Oh, he excels at that, sir.

INT. LARS HOMESTEAD – PLAZA

Morning slowly creeps into the sparse but sparkling oasis of the open courtyard. The idyll is broken by the yelling of Uncle Owen, his voice echoing throughout the homestead.

OWEN

Luke? Luke? Luke? Where could he be loafing now!?

INT. LARS HOMESTEAD – KITCHEN

The interior of the kitchen is a warm glow as Aunt Beru prepares the morning breakfast. Owen enters in a huff.

OWEN

Have you seen Luke this morning?

AUNT BERU

He said he had some things to do before he started today, so he left early.

OWEN

Uh? Did he take those two new droids with him?

AUNT BERU

I think so.

OWEN

Well, he'd better have those units in the south range repaired by midday or there'll be hell to pay!

EXT. TATOOINE DESERT WASTELAND – LUKE'S SPEEDER – DAY

The rock and sand of the desert floor are a blur as Threepio pilots the sleek landspeeder gracefully across the vast wasteland.

INT./EXT. LUKE'S SPEEDER – DESERT WASTELAND – TRAVELING – DAY

Luke leans over the back of the speeder and adjusts something in the motor compartment.

LUKE
(*yelling*)

How's that?

Threepio signals that it is fine and Luke turns back into the wind-whipped cockpit and pops the canopy shut.

LUKE

Old Ben Kenobi lives out in this direction somewhere, but I

36

don't see how that R2 unit could have come this far. We must have missed him. Uncle Owen isn't going to take this very well.

THREEPIO

Sir, would it help if you told him it was my fault?

LUKE
(*brightening*)
Sure. He needs you. He'd probably only deactivate you for a day or so . . .

THREEPIO

Deactivate! Well, on the other hand, if you hadn't removed his restraining bolt . . .

LUKE

Wait, there's something dead ahead on the scanner. It looks like our droid . . . hit the accelerator.

EXT. TATOOINE — ROCK MESA — DUNE SEA — COASTLINE — DAY

From high on a rock mesa, the tiny landspeeder can be seen gliding across the desert floor. Suddenly, in the foreground two weather-beaten Sand People shrouded in their grimy desert cloaks peer over the edge of the rock mesa. One of the marginally human creatures raises a long ominous laser rifle and points it at the speeder but the second creature grabs the gun before it can be fired.

The Sand People, or Tusken Raiders as they're sometimes called, speak in a coarse barbaric language as they get into an animated argument. The second Tusken Raider seems to get in the final word and the nomads scurry over the rocky terrain.

EXT. TATOOINE — ROCK MESA — CANYON

The Tusken Raiders approach two large banthas standing tied to a rock. The monstrous, bear-like creatures are as large as elephants, with huge red eyes, tremendous looped horns, and long, furry, dinosaur-like tails. The Tusken Raiders mount saddles strapped to the huge creatures' shaggy backs and ride off down the rugged bluff.

The speeder is parked on the floor of a massive canyon. Luke, with his long laser rifle slung over his shoulder, stands before little Artoo.

LUKE

Hey, whoa, just where do you think you're going?

The little droid whistles a feeble reply, as Threepio poses menacingly behind the little runaway.

THREEPIO

Master Luke here is your rightful owner. We'll have no more of this Obi-Wan Kenobi gibberish . . . and don't talk to me of your mission, either. You're fortunate he doesn't blast you into a million pieces right here.

LUKE

Well, come on. It's getting late. I only hope we can get back before Uncle Owen really blows up.

THREEPIO

If you don't mind my saying so, sir, I think you should deactivate the little fugitive until you've gotten him back to your workshop.

LUKE

No, he's not going to try anything.

Suddenly the little robot jumps to life with a mass of frantic whistles and screams.

LUKE

What's wrong with him now?

THREEPIO

Oh my . . . sir, he says there are several creatures approaching from the southeast.

Luke swings his rifle into position and looks to the south.

LUKE

Sand People! Or worse! Come on, let's go have a look. Come on.

EXT. TATOOINE – ROCK CANYON – RIDGE – DAY

Luke carefully makes his way to the top of a rock ridge and scans the canyon with his electrobinoculars.

He spots the two riderless banthas. Threepio struggles up behind the young adventurer.

> **LUKE**
>
> There are two banthas down there but I don't see any . . . wait a second, they're Sand People all right. I can see one of them now.

Luke watches the distant Tusken Raider through his electrobinoculars. Suddenly, something huge moves in front of his field of view. Before Luke or Threepio can react, a large, gruesome Tusken Raider looms over them. Threepio is startled and backs away, right off the side of the cliff. He can be heard for several moments as he clangs, bangs and rattles down the side of the mountain.

The towering creature brings down his curved, double-pointed gaderffii – the dreaded axe blade that has struck terror in the heart of the local settlers. But Luke manages to block the blow with his laser rifle, which is smashed to pieces. The terrified farm boy scrambles backward until he is forced to the edge of a deep crevice. The sinister Raider stands over him with his weapon raised and lets out a horrible shrieking laugh.

EXT. TATOOINE – ROCK CANYON FLOOR – DAY

Artoo forces himself into the shadows of a small alcove in the rocks as the vicious Sand People walk past carrying the inert Luke Skywalker, who is dropped in a heap before the speeder. The Sand People ransack the speeder, throwing parts and supplies in all directions. Suddenly, they stop. Then everything is quiet for a few moments. A great howling moan is heard throughout the canyon which sends the Sand People fleeing in terror.

Artoo moves even tighter into the shadows as the slight swishing sound that frightened off the Sand People grows even closer, until a shabby old desert-rat-of-a-man appears and leans over Luke. His ancient leathery face, cracked and weathered by exotic climates, is set off by dark, penetrating eyes and a scraggly white beard. Ben Kenobi squints his eyes as he scrutinizes the unconscious farm boy. Artoo makes a slight sound and Ben turns and looks right at him.

BEN
Hello there! Come here, my little friend. Don't be afraid.

Artoo waddles over to where Luke lies crumpled in a heap and begins to whistle and beep his concern. Ben puts his hand on Luke's forehead and he begins to come around.

BEN

Don't worry, he'll be all right.

LUKE

What happened?

BEN

Rest easy, son, you've had a busy day. You're fortunate you're still in one piece.

LUKE

Ben? Ben Kenobi! Boy, am I glad to see you!

BEN

The Jundland Wastes are not to be traveled lightly. Tell me, young Luke, what brings you out this far?

LUKE

Oh, this little droid! I think he's searching for his former master . . . I've never seen such devotion in a droid before . . . there seems to be no stopping him. He claims to be the property of an Obi-Wan Kenobi. Is he a relative of yours? Do you know who he's talking about?

Ben ponders this for a moment, scratching his scruffy beard.

BEN

Obi-Wan Kenobi . . . Obi-Wan? Now that's a name I haven't heard in a long time . . . a long time.

LUKE

I think my uncle knew him. He said he was dead . . .

BEN

Oh, he's not dead, no . . . not yet.

LUKE

You know him!

BEN

Well of course, of course I know him. He's me! I haven't

gone by the name Obi-Wan since, oh, before you were
born.

LUKE

Then this droid does belong to you.

BEN

Don't seem to remember ever owning a droid. Very
interesting . . .

He suddenly looks up at the overhanging cliffs.

BEN

I think we better get indoors. The Sand People are easily
startled but they will soon be back and in greater numbers.

*Luke sits up and rubs his head. Artoo lets out a pathetic beep, causing
Luke to remember something. He looks around.*

LUKE

Threepio!

EXT. TATOOINE – SAND P   ROCK MESA – DAY

*Little Artoo stands at the edge of a large sand pit and begins to chatter
away in electronic whistles and beeps. Luke and Ben stand over a very
dented and tangled Threepio lying half-buried in the sand. One of his
arms has broken off.*

*Luke tries to revive the inert robot by shaking him and then flips a
hidden switch on h* `ack several times until finally the mechanical
man's systems turn on.*

THREEPIO

Where am I? I must have taken a bad step . . .

LUKE

Can you stand? We've got to get out of here before the Sand
People return.

THREEPIO

I don't think I can make it. You go on, Master Luke. There's
no sense in you risking yourself on my account. I'm done for.

Artoo makes a beeping sound.

42

LUKE

No, you're not. What kind of talk is that?

Luke and Ben help the battered robot to his feet. Little Artoo watches from the top of the pit. Ben glances around suspiciously. Sensing something, he stands up and sniffs the air.

BEN

Quickly, son . . . they're on the move.

INT. KENOBI'S DWELLING

The small, spartan hovel is cluttered with desert junk but still manages to radiate an air of time-worn comfort and security. Luke is in one corner repairing Threepio's arm, as old Ben sits thinking.

LUKE

No, my father didn't fight in the wars. He was a navigator on a spice freighter.

BEN

That's what your uncle told you. He didn't hold with your father's ideals. Thought he should have stayed here and not gotten involved.

LUKE

You fought in the Clone Wars?

BEN

Yes. I was once a Jedi Knight the same as your father.

LUKE

I wish I'd known him.

BEN

He was the best star-pilot in the galaxy, and a cunning warrior. I understand you've become quite a good pilot yourself. And he was a good friend. Which reminds me . . .

Ben gets up and goes to a chest where he rummages around. As Luke finishes repairing Threepio and starts to fit the restraining bolt back on, Threepio looks at him nervously. Luke thinks about the bolt for a moment then puts it on the table. Ben shuffles up and presents Luke with a short handle with several electronic gadgets attached to it.

43

BEN

I have something here for you. Your father wanted you to
have this when you were old enough, but your uncle wouldn't
allow it. He feared you might follow old Obi-Wan on some
damned-fool idealistic crusade like your father did.

THREEPIO

Sir, if you'll not be needing me, I'll close down for a while.

LUKE

Sure, go ahead.

Ben hands Luke the saber.

LUKE

What is it?

BEN

Your father's lightsaber. This is the weapon of a Jedi Knight.
Not as clumsy or as random as a blaster.

*Luke pushes a button on the handle. A long beam shoots out about four
feet and flickers there. The light plays across the ceiling.*

BEN

An elegant weapon for a more civilized time. For over a
thousand generations the Jedi Knights were the guardians of
peace and justice in the Old Republic. Before the dark times,
before the Empire.

Luke hasn't really been listening.

LUKE

How did my father die?

BEN

A young Jedi named Darth Vader, who was a pupil of mine
until he turned to evil, helped the Empire hunt down and
destroy the Jedi Knights. He betrayed and murdered your
father. Now the Jedi are all but extinct. Vader was seduced by
the dark side of the Force.

LUKE

The Force?

BEN

Well, the Force is what gives the Jedi his power. It's an energy field created by all living things. It surrounds us and penetrates us. It binds the galaxy together.

Artoo makes beeping sounds.

BEN

Now, let's see if we can't figure out what you are, my little friend. And where you come from.

LUKE

I saw part of the message he was . . .

Luke is cut short as the recorded image of the beautiful young Rebel princess is projected from Artoo's face.

BEN

I seem to have found it.

Luke stops his work as the lovely girl's image flickers before his eyes.

LEIA

General Kenobi, years ago you served my father in the Clone Wars. Now he begs you to help him in his struggle against the Empire. I regret that I am unable to present my father's request to you in person, but my ship has fallen under attack and I'm afraid my mission to bring you to Alderaan has failed. I have placed information vital to the survival of the Rebellion into the memory systems of this R2 unit. My father will know how to retrieve it. You must see this droid safely delivered to him on Alderaan. This is our most desperate hour. Help me, Obi-Wan Kenobi, you're my only hope.

There is a little static and the transmission is cut short. Old Ben leans back and scratches his head. He silently puffs on a tarnished chrome water pipe. Luke has stars in his eyes.

BEN

You must learn the ways of the Force if you're to come with me to Alderaan.

LUKE
(*laughing*)

Alderaan? I'm not going to Alderaan. I've got to go home. It's
late, I'm in for it as it is.

BEN

I need your help, Luke. She needs your help. I'm getting too
old for this sort of thing.

LUKE

I can't get involved! I've got work to do! It's not that I like the
Empire. I hate it! But there's nothing I can do about it right
now. It's such a long way from here.

BEN

That's your uncle talking.

LUKE
(*sighing*)

Oh, God, my uncle. How am I ever going to explain this?

BEN

Learn about the Force, Luke.

LUKE

Look, I can take you as far as Anchorhead. You can get a
transport there to Mos Eisley or wherever you're going.

BEN

You must do what you feel is right, of course.

EXT. SPACE

*An Imperial Star Destroyer heads towards the evil planet-like battle
station: the Death Star!*

INT. DEATH STAR – CONFERENCE ROOM

*Eight Imperial senators and generals sit around a black conference table.
Imperial stormtroopers stand guard around the room. Commander
Tagge, a young, slimy-looking general, is speaking.*

TAGGE

Until this battle station is fully operational we are vulnerable.

The Rebel Alliance is too well equipped. They're more dangerous than you realize.

The bitter Admiral Motti twists nervously in his chair.

MOTTI

Dangerous to your starfleet, Commander; not to this battle station!

TAGGE

The Rebellion will continue to gain support in the Imperial Senate as long as . . .

Suddenly all heads turn as Commander Tagge's speech is cut short and the Grand Moff Tarkin, governor of the Imperial outland regions, enters. He is followed by his powerful ally, the Sith Lord, Darth Vader. All of the generals stand and bow before the thin, evil-looking governor as he takes his place at the head of the table. The Dark Lord stands behind him.

TARKIN

The Imperial Senate will no longer be of any concern to us. I've just received word that the Emperor has dissolved the council permanently. The last remnants of the Old Republic have been swept away.

TAGGE

That's impossible! How will the Emperor maintain control without the bureaucracy?

TARKIN

The regional governors now have direct control over territories. Fear will keep the local systems in line. Fear of this battle station.

TAGGE

And what of the Rebellion? If the Rebels have obtained a complete technical readout of this station, it is possible, however unlikely, that they might find a weakness and exploit it.

VADER

The plans you refer to will soon be back in our hands.

47

MOTTI

Any attack made by the Rebels against this station would be a useless gesture, no matter what technical data they've obtained. This station is now the ultimate power in the universe. I suggest we use it!

VADER

Don't be too proud of this technological terror you've constructed. The ability to destroy a planet is insignificant next to the power of the Force.

MOTTI

Don't try to frighten us with your sorcerer's ways, Lord Vader. Your sad devotion to that ancient religion has not helped you conjure up the stolen data tapes, or given you clairvoyance enough to find the Rebels' hidden fort . . .

Suddenly Motti chokes and starts to turn blue under Vader's spell.

VADER

I find your lack of faith disturbing.

TARKIN

Enough of this! Vader, release him!

VADER

As you wish.

TARKIN

This bickering is pointless. Lord Vader will provide us with the location of the Rebel fortress by the time this station is operational. We will then crush the Rebellion with one swift stroke.

EXT. TATOOINE – WASTELAND

The speeder stops before what remains of the huge Jawa sandcrawler. Luke and Ben walk among the smoldering rubble and scattered bodies.

LUKE

It looks like Sand People did this, all right. Look, here are gaffi sticks, bantha tracks. It's just . . . I never heard of them hitting anything this big before.

48

Ben is crouching in the sand studying the tracks.

BEN

They didn't. But we are meant to think they did. These tracks are side by side. Sand People always ride single file to hide their numbers.

LUKE

These are the same Jawas that sold us Artoo and Threepio.

BEN

And these blast points, too accurate for Sand People. Only Imperial stormtroopers are so precise.

LUKE

Why would Imperial troops want to slaughter Jawas?

He looks back at the speeder where Artoo and Threepio are inspecting the dead Jawas, and puts two and two together.

LUKE

If they traced the robots here, they may have learned who they sold them to. And that would lead them back home!

He reaches a sudden horrible realization, then races for the speeder and jumps in.

BEN

Wait, Luke! It's too dangerous.

Luke races off, leaving Ben and the two robots alone with the burning sandcrawler.

EXT. TATOOINE — WASTELAND

Luke races across the flat landscape in his battered landspeeder.

EXT. TATOOINE — LARS HOMESTEAD

The speeder roars up to the homestead.

Luke jumps out and runs to the smoking holes that were once his home. Debris is scattered everywhere and it looks as if a great battle has taken place.

LUKE
Uncle Owen! Aunt Beru! Uncle Owen!

Luke stumbles around in a daze looking for his aunt and uncle. Suddenly, he comes upon their smoldering remains. He is stunned, and cannot speak. Hate replaces fear and a new resolve comes over him.

EXT. SPACE

Imperial TIE fighters race towards the Death Star.

INT. DEATH STAR — DETENTION CORRIDOR

Two stormtroopers open an electronic cell door and allow several Imperial guards to enter. Princess Leia's face is filled with defiance, which slowly gives way to fear as a giant black torture robot enters, followed by Darth Vader.

VADER
And now, Your Highness, we will discuss the location of your hidden Rebel base.

The torture robot gives off a steady beeping sound as it approaches Princess Leia and extends one of its mechanical arms bearing a large hypodermic needle. The door slides shut and the long cell block hallway appears peaceful. The muffled screams of the Rebel princess are barely heard.

EXT. TATOOINE — WASTELAND

There is a large bonfire of Jawa bodies blazing in front of the sandcrawler as Ben and the robots finish burning the dead. Luke drives up in the speeder and Ben walks over to him.

BEN
There's nothing you could have done, Luke, had you been there. You'd have been killed, too, and the droids would now be in the hands of the Empire.

LUKE
I want to come with you to Alderaan. There's nothing here for me now. I want to learn the ways of the Force and become a Jedi like my father.

EXT. TATOOINE — WASTELAND

The landspeeder with Luke, Artoo, Threepio, and Ben in it zooms across the desert. The speeder stops on a bluff overlooking the spaceport at Mos Eisley. It is a haphazard array of low, gray, concrete structures and semi-domes. A harsh gale blows across the stark canyon floor. Luke adjusts his goggles and walks to the edge of the craggy bluff where Ben is standing.

> BEN
>
> Mos Eisley Spaceport. You will never find a more wretched hive of scum and villainy. We must be cautious.

He looks over at Luke, who gives the old Jedi a determined smile.

EXT. TATOOINE — MOS EISLEY — STREET

The speeder is stopped on a crowded street by several combat-hardened stormtroopers who look over the two robots. A trooper questions Luke.

> TROOPER
>
> How long have you had these droids?

> LUKE
>
> About three or four seasons.

> BEN
>
> They're for sale if you want them.

> TROOPER
>
> Let me see your identification.

Luke becomes very nervous as he fumbles to find his ID while Ben speaks to the trooper in a very controlled voice.

> BEN
>
> You don't need to see his identification.

> TROOPER
>
> We don't need to see his identification.

> BEN
>
> These are not the droids you're looking for.

> TROOPER

These are not the droids we're looking for.

> BEN

He can go about his business.

> TROOPER

You can go about your business.

> BEN
> (*to Luke*)

Move along.

> TROOPER

Move along. Move along.

EXT. TATOOINE – MOS EISLEY – STREET

The speeder pulls up in front of a rundown blockhouse cantina on the outskirts of the spaceport. Various strange forms of transport, including several unusual beasts of burden, are parked outside the bar. A Jawa runs up and begins to fondle the speeder.

> THREEPIO

I can't abide these Jawas. Disgusting creatures.

As Luke gets out of the speeder he tries to shoo the Jawa away.

> LUKE

Go on, go on. I can't understand how we got by those troopers. I thought we were dead.

> BEN

The Force can have a strong influence on the weak-minded. You will find it a powerful ally.

> LUKE

Do you really think we're going to find a pilot here that'll take us to Alderaan?

> BEN

Well, most of the best freighter pilots can be found here. Only watch your step. This place can be a little rough.

LUKE

I'm ready for anything.

THREEPIO

Come along, Artoo.

INT. TATOOINE — MOS EISLEY — CANTINA

The young adventurer and his two mechanical servants follow Ben Kenobi into the smoke-filled cantina. The murky, moldy den is filled with a startling array of weird and exotic alien creatures and monsters at the long metallic bar. At first the sight is horrifying. One-eyed, thousand-eyed, slimy, furry, scaly, tentacled, and clawed creatures huddle over drinks. Ben moves to an empty spot at the bar near a group of repulsive but human scum. A huge, rough-looking Bartender stops Luke and the robots.

BARTENDER

We don't serve their kind here!

Luke, still recovering from the shock of seeing so many outlandish creatures, doesn't quite catch the bartender's drift.

LUKE

What?

BARTENDER

Your droids. They'll have to wait outside. We don't want them here.

Luke looks to old Ben, who is busy talking to one of the galactic pirates. He notices that several of the gruesome creatures along the bar are giving him a very unfriendly glare.

Luke pats Threepio on the shoulder.

LUKE

Listen, why don't you wait out by the speeder. We don't want any trouble.

THREEPIO

I heartily agree with you, sir.

Threepio and his stubby partner go outside and most of the creatures at the bar go back to their drinks.

Ben is standing next to Chewbacca, an eight-foot-tall savage-looking creature resembling a huge gray bushbaby monkey with fierce baboon-like fangs. His large blue eyes dominate a fur-covered face and soften his otherwise awesome appearance. Over his matted, furry body he wears two chrome bandoliers, and little else. He is a two hundred-year-old Wookiee and a sight to behold.

Ben speaks to the Wookiee, pointing to Luke several times during his conversation, and the huge creature suddenly lets out a horrifying laugh. Luke is more than a little disconcerted and pretends not to hear the conversation between Ben and the giant Wookiee.

Luke is terrified but tries not to show it. He quietly sips his drink, looking over the crowd for a more sympathetic ear or whatever.

A large, multiple-eyed Creature gives Luke a rough shove.

CREATURE

Negola dewaghi wooldugger!?

The hideous freak is obviously drunk. Luke tries to ignore the creature and turns back to his drink. A short, grubby Human and an even smaller rodent-like beast join the belligerent monstrosity.

HUMAN

He doesn't like you.

LUKE

I'm sorry.

HUMAN

I don't like you either.

The big creature is getting agitated and yells some unintelligible gibberish at the now rather nervous young adventurer.

Don't insult us. You just watch yourself. We're wanted men. I have the death sentence on twelve systems.

LUKE

I'll be careful then.

HUMAN

You'll be dead.

The rodent lets out a loud grunt and everything at the bar moves away. Luke tries to remain cool but it isn't easy. His three adversaries ready their weapons. Old Ben moves in behind Luke.

BEN

This little one isn't worth the effort. Come, let me buy you something.

A powerful blow from the unpleasant creature sends the young would-be Jedi sailing across the room, crashing through tables and breaking a large jug filled with a foul-looking liquid. With a blood-curdling shriek, the monster draws a wicked chrome laser pistol from his belt and levels it at old Ben. The bartender panics.

BARTENDER

No blasters! No blasters!

With astounding agility old Ben's laser sword sparks to life and in a

flash an arm lies on the floor. The rodent is cut in two and the giant multiple-eyed creature lies doubled, cut from chin to groin. Ben carefully and precisely turns off his laser sword and replaces it on his utility belt. Luke, shaking and totally amazed at the old man's abilities, attempts to stand. The entire fight has lasted only a matter of seconds. The cantina goes back to normal, although Ben is given a respectable amount of room at the bar. Luke, rubbing his bruised head, approaches the old man with new awe. Ben points to the Wookiee.

BEN

This is Chewbacca. He's first mate on a ship that might suit our needs.

EXT. TATOOINE – MOS EISLEY – STREET

Threepio paces in front of the cantina as Artoo carries on an electronic conversation with another little red astro-droid. The creature comes out of the cantina and approaches two stormtroopers in the street.

THREEPIO

I don't like the look of this.

INT. TATOOINE – MOS EISLEY – CANTINA

Strange creatures play exotic big-band music on odd-looking instruments as Luke, still giddy, downs a fresh drink and follows Ben and Chewbacca to a booth where Han Solo is sitting. Han is a tough, roguish starpilot, about thirty years old. A mercenary on a starship, he is simple, sentimental, and cocksure.

HAN

Han Solo. I'm captain of the *Millennium Falcon*. Chewie here tells me you're looking for passage to the Alderaan system.

BEN

Yes, indeed. If it's a fast ship.

HAN

Fast ship? You've never heard of the *Millennium Falcon*?

BEN

Should I have?

HAN

It's the ship that made the Kessel run in less than twelve
parsecs!

*Ben reacts to Solo's stupid attempt to impress them with obvious
misinformation.*

HAN

I've outrun Imperial starships, not the local bulk-cruisers,
mind you. I'm talking about the big Corellian ships now.
She's fast enough for you, old man. What's the cargo?

BEN

Only passengers. Myself, the boy, two droids, and no
questions asked.

HAN

What is it? Some kind of local trouble?

BEN

Let's just say we'd like to avoid any Imperial entanglements.

HAN

Well, that's the real trick, isn't it? And it's going to cost you
something extra. Ten thousand in advance.

LUKE

Ten thousand? We could almost buy our own ship for that!

HAN

But who's going to fly it, kid! You?

LUKE

You bet I could. I'm not such a bad pilot myself! We don't
have to sit here and listen . . .

BEN

We haven't that much with us. But we could pay you two
thousand now, plus fifteen when we reach Alderaan.

HAN

Seventeen, huh!

He ponders this for a few moments.

HAN

Okay. You guys got yourself a ship. We'll leave as soon as you're ready. Docking Bay Ninety-four.

BEN

Ninety-four.

HAN

Looks like somebody's beginning to take an interest in your handiwork.

Ben and Luke turn around to see four Imperial stormtroopers looking at the dead bodies and asking the bartender some questions. The bartender points to the booth.

TROOPER

All right, we'll check it out.

The stormtroopers look over at the booth but Luke and Ben are gone. The bartender shrugs his shoulders in puzzlement.

HAN
(*to Chewbacca*)

Seventeen thousand! Those guys must really be desperate. This could really save my neck. Get back to the ship and get her ready.

EXT. TATOOINE – MOS EISLEY – STREET

BEN

You'll have to sell your speeder.

LUKE

That's okay. I'm never coming back to this planet again.

INT. MOS EISLEY – CANTINA

As Han is about to leave, Greedo, a slimy green-faced alien with a short trunk-nose, pokes a gun in his side. The creature speaks in a foreign tongue translated into English subtitles.

GREEDO

Going somewhere, Solo?

Yes, Greedo. As a matter of fact, I was just going to see your boss. Tell Jabba that I've got his money.

Han sits down and the alien sits across from him holding the gun on him.

GREEDO

It's too late. You should have paid him when you had the chance. Jabba's put a price on your head, so large that every bounty hunter in the galaxy will be looking for you. I'm lucky I found you first.

HAN

Yeah, but this time I got the money.

GREEDO

If you give it to me, I might forget I found you.

HAN

I don't have it with me. Tell Jabba . . .

GREEDO

Jabba's through with you. He has no time for smugglers who drop their shipments at the first sign of an Imperial cruiser.

HAN

Even I get boarded sometimes. Do you think I had a choice?

Han Solo slowly reaches for his gun under the table.

GREEDO

You can tell that to Jabba. He may only take your ship.

HAN

Over my dead body.

GREEDO

'That's the idea. I've been looking forward to killing you for a long time.

HAN

Yes, I'll bet you have.

Suddenly, the slimy alien disappears in a blinding flash of light. Han pulls his smoking gun from beneath the table as the other patrons look on in bemused amazement. Han gets up and starts out of the cantina, flipping the bartender some coins as he leaves.

> HAN
>
> Sorry about the mess.

EXT. SPACE

Several TIE fighters approach the Death Star.

INT. DEATH STAR — CONTROL ROOM

> VADER
>
> Her resistance to the mind probe is considerable. It will be some time before we can extract any information from her.

An Imperial Officer interrupts the meeting.

> IMPERIAL OFFICER
>
> The final check-out is completed. All systems are operational. What course shall we set?

> TARKIN
>
> Perhaps she would respond to an alternative form of persuasion.

> VADER
>
> What do you mean?

> TARKIN
>
> I think it is time we demonstrated the full power of this station.
> *(to Trooper)*
> Set your course for Princess Leia's home planet of Alderaan.

> TROOPER
>
> With pleasure.

EXT. TATOOINE — MOS EISLEY — STREET

Four heavily armed stormtroopers move menacingly along a narrow slum alleyway crowded with darkly clad creatures hawking exotic goods in dingy little stalls. Men, monsters, and robots crouch in waste-filled doorways, whispering and hiding from the hot winds.

> **THREEPIO**
> Lock the door, Artoo.

One of the troopers checks a tightly locked door and moves on down the alleyway. The door slides open a crack and Threepio peeks out. Artoo is barely visible in the background.

> **TROOPER**
> All right, check that side of the street. It's secure. Move on to the next one.

The door opens. Threepio moves into the doorway.

> **THREEPIO**
> I would much rather have gone with Master Luke than stay here with you. I don't know what all this trouble is about, but I'm sure it must be your fault.

Artoo makes beeping sounds.

> **THREEPIO**
> You watch your language!

EXT. TATOOINE – MOS EISLEY – STREET – ALLEYWAY – USED-SPEEDER LOT

Ben and Luke are standing in a sleazy used speeder lot, talking with a tall, grotesque, insect-like used-speeder dealer. Strange exotic bodies and spindly-legged beasts pass by as the insect concludes the sale by giving Luke some coins.

> **LUKE**
> He says it's the best he can do. Since the XP-38 came out, they just aren't in demand.

> **BEN**
> It will be enough.

Ben and Luke leave the speeder lot and walk down the dusty alleyway past a small robot herding a bunch of anteater-like creatures. Luke turns and gives one last forlorn look at his faithful speeder as he rounds a corner. A darkly clad creature moves out of the shadows as they pass and watches them as they disappear down another alley.

BEN

If the ship's as fast as he's boasting, we ought to do well.

INT. DOCKING BAY 94 – DAY

Jabba the Hutt and a half-dozen grisly alien pirates and purple creatures stand in the middle of the docking bay. Jabba is the grossest of the slavering hulks and his scarred face is a grim testimonial to his prowess as a vicious killer. He is a fat, slug-like creature with eyes on extended feelers and a huge ugly mouth.

JABBA

Come on out, Solo!

A voice from directly behind the pirates startles them and they turn around to see Han Solo and the giant Wookiee, Chewbacca, standing behind them with no weapons in sight.

HAN

I've been waiting for you, Jabba.

JABBA

I expected you would be.

HAN

I'm not the type to run.

JABBA
(fatherly smooth)

Han, my boy, there are times when you disappoint me . . . why haven't you paid me? And why did you have to fry poor Greedo like that . . . after all we've been through together.

HAN

You sent Greedo to blast me.

JABBA
(mock surprise)

Han, why, you're the best smuggler in the business. You're too valuable to fry. He was only relaying my concern at your delays. He wasn't going to blast you.

HAN

I think he thought he was. Next time don't send one of those twerps. If you've got something to say to me, come see me yourself.

JABBA

Han, Han! If only you hadn't had to dump that shipment of spice . . . you understand I just can't make an exception. Where would I be if every pilot who smuggled for me dumped their shipment at the first sign of an Imperial starship? It's not good business.

HAN

You know, even I get boarded sometimes, Jabba. I had no choice, but I've got a charter now and I can pay you back, plus a little extra. I just need some more time.

JABBA
(*to his men*)

Put your blasters away. Han, my boy, I'm only doing this because you're the best and I need you. So, for an extra, say . . . twenty percent I'll give you a little more time . . . but this is it. If you disappoint me again, I'll put a price on your head so large you won't be able to go near a civilized system for the rest of your short life.

HAN

Jabba, I'll pay you because it's my pleasure.

EXT. DOCKING PORT ENTRY – ALLEYWAY

Chewbacca waits restlessly at the entrance to Docking Bay 94. Ben, Luke, and the robots make their way up the street. Chewbacca jabbers excitedly and signals for them to hurry. The darkly clad creature has followed them from the speeder lot. He stops in a nearby doorway and speaks into a small transmitter.

INT. MOS EISLEY SPACEPORT – DOCKING BAY 94

Chewbacca leads the group into the giant dirt pit that is Docking Bay 94. Resting in the middle of the huge hole is a large, round, beat-up, pieced-together hunk of junk that could only loosely be called a starship.

LUKE

What a piece of junk.

The tall figure of Han Solo comes down the boarding ramp.

HAN

She'll make point five beyond the speed of light. She may not look like much, but she's got it where it counts, kid. I've added some special modifications myself.

Luke scratches his head. It's obvious he isn't sure about all this. Chewbacca rushes up the ramp and urges the others to follow.

HAN

We're a little rushed, so if you'll hurry aboard we'll get out of here.

The group rushes up the gangplank, passing a grinning Han Solo.

INT. *MILLENNIUM FALCON*

Chewbacca settles into the pilot's chair and starts the mighty engines of the starship.

INT. MOS EISLEY SPACE PORT – DOCKING BAY 94

Luke, Ben, Threepio, and Artoo move toward the Millenium Falcon *passing Solo.*

THREEPIO

Hello, sir.

EXT. TATOOINE – MOS EISLEY – STREET

Eight Imperial stormtroopers rush up to the darkly clad creature.

TROOPER

Which way?

The darkly clad creature points to the door of the docking bay.

TROOPER

All right, men. Load your weapons!

INT. MOS EISLEY SPACEPORT — DOCKING BAY 94

The troops hold their guns at the ready and charge down the docking bay entrance.

TROOPER
Stop that ship!

Han Solo looks up and sees the Imperial stormtroopers rushing into the docking bay. Several of the troopers fire at Han as he ducks into the spaceship.

TROOPER
Blast 'em!

Han draws his laser pistol and pops off a couple of shots which force the stormtroopers to dive for safety. The pirateship engines whine as Han hits the release button that slams the overhead entry shut.

INT. *MILLENNIUM FALCON*

HAN
Chewie, get us out of here!

The group straps in for takeoff.

THREEPIO
Oh, my, I'd forgotten how much I hate space travel.

EXT. TATOOINE — MOS EISLEY — STREETS

The half-dozen stormtroopers at a checkpoint hear the general alarm and look to the sky as the huge starship rises above the dingy slum dwellings and quickly disappears into the morning sky.

INT. *MILLENNIUM FALCON* — COCKPIT

Han climbs into the pilot's chair next to Chewbacca, who chatters away as he points to something on the radar scope.

EXT. SPACE — PLANET TATOOINE

Han frantically types information into the ship's computer. Little Artoo appears momentarily at the cockpit doorway, makes a few beeping remarks, then scurries away.

HAN

It looks like an Imperial cruiser. Our passengers must be hotter than I thought. Try and hold them off. Angle the deflector shield while I make the calculations for the jump to light speed.

EXT. SPACE – PLANET TATOOINE

The Millennium Falcon *pirateship races away from the yellow planet. It is followed by two huge Imperial Star Destroyers.*

INT. *MILLENNIUM FALCON* – COCKPIT

Over the shoulders of Chewbacca and Han, we can see the galaxy spread before them. Luke and Ben make their way into the cramped cockpit where Han continues his calculation.

HAN

Stay sharp! There are two more coming in; they're going to try to cut us off.

LUKE

Why don't you outrun them? I thought you said this thing was fast.

HAN

Watch your mouth, kid, or you're going to find yourself floating home. We'll be safe enough once we make the jump to hyperspace. Besides, I know a few maneuvers. We'll lose them!

EXT. SPACE – PLANET TATOOINE

Imperial cruisers fire at the pirateship.

INT. *MILLENNIUM FALCON* – COCKPIT

The ship shudders as an explosion flashes outside the window.

HAN

Here's where the fun begins!

BEN

How long before you can make the jump to light speed?

HAN

It'll take a few moments to get the coordinates from the navi-computer.

The ship begins to rock violently as lasers hit it.

LUKE

Are you kidding? At the rate they're gaining . . .

HAN

Traveling through hyperspace isn't like dusting crops, boy! Without precise calculations we could fly right through a star or bounce too close to a supernova and that'd end your trip real quick, wouldn't it?

The ship is now constantly battered with laserfire as a red warning light begins to flash.

LUKE

What's that flashing?

HAN

We're losing our deflector shield. Go strap yourself in. I'm going to make the jump to light speed.

The galaxy brightens and they move faster, almost as if crashing a barrier. Stars become streaks as the pirateship makes the jump to hyperspace.

EXT. SPACE

The Millennium Falcon *zooms into infinity in less than a second.*

EXT. DEATH STAR

Alderaan looms behind the Death Star battle station.

INT. DEATH STAR — CONTROL ROOM

Admiral Motti enters the quiet control room and bows before Governor Tarkin, who stands before the huge wall screen displaying a small green planet.

MOTTI

We've entered the Alderaan system.

Vader and two stormtroopers enter with Princess Leia. Her hands are bound.

LEIA

Governor Tarkin. I should have expected to find you holding Vader's leash. I recognized your foul stench when I was brought on board.

TARKIN

Charming to the last. You don't know how hard I found it signing the order to terminate your life!

LEIA

I'm surprised you had the courage to take the responsibility yourself!

TARKIN

Princess Leia, before your execution I would like you to be my guest at a ceremony that will make this battle station operational. No star system will dare oppose the Emperor now.

LEIA

The more you tighten your grip, Tarkin, the more star systems will slip through your fingers.

TARKIN

Not after we demonstrate the power of this station. In a way, you have determined the choice of the planet that'll be destroyed first. Since you are reluctant to provide us with the location of the Rebel base, I have chosen to test this station's destructive power . . . on your home planet of Alderaan.

LEIA

No! Alderaan is peaceful. We have no weapons. You can't possibly . . .

TARKIN

You would prefer another target? A military target? Then name the system!

He waves menacingly towards Leia.

TARKIN

I grow tired of asking this. So it'll be the last time. Where is the Rebel base?

Leia overhears an intercom voice announcing the approach to Alderaan.

LEIA
(*softly*)

Dantooine.

She lowers her head.

LEIA

They're on Dantooine.

TARKIN

There. You see, Lord Vader, she can be reasonable.
(*to Motti*)
Continue with the operation. You may fire when ready.

LEIA

What?

TARKIN

You're far too trusting. Dantooine is too remote to make an effective demonstration. But don't worry. We will deal with your Rebel friends soon enough.

LEIA

No!

INT. DEATH STAR – BLAST CHAMBER

VADER

Commence primary ignition.

A button is pressed which switches on a panel of lights. A hooded Imperial soldier reaches overhead and pulls a lever. Another lever is pulled. Vader reaches for still another lever and a bank of lights on a panel and wall lights up. A huge beam of light emanates from within a cone-shaped area and converges into a single laser beam out towards Alderaan. The small green planet of Alderaan is blown into space dust.

Ben watches as Luke practices the lightsaber with a small 'seeker' robot. Ben suddenly turns away and sits down. He falters, seems almost faint.

LUKE

Are you all right? What's wrong?

BEN

I felt a great disturbance in the Force . . . as if millions of voices suddenly cried out in terror and were suddenly silenced. I fear something terrible has happened.

Ben rubs his forehead and seems to drift into a trance. Then he fixes his gaze on Luke.

BEN

You'd better get on with your exercises.

Han Solo enters the room.

HAN

Well, you can forget your troubles with those Imperial slugs. I told you I'd outrun 'em.

Luke is once again practicing with the lightsaber.

HAN

Don't everybody thank me at once.

Threepio watches Chewbacca and Artoo who are engrossed in a game in which three-dimensional holographic figures move along a chess-type board.

HAN

Anyway, we should be at Alderaan about oh-two-hundred hours.

Chewbacca and the two robots sit around the lighted table covered with small holographic monsters. Each side of the table has a small computer monitor embedded in it. Chewbacca seems very pleased with himself as he rests his lanky fur-covered arms over his head.

THREEPIO

Now be careful, Artoo.

*Artoo immediately reaches up and taps the computer with his stubby
claw hand, causing one of the holographic creatures to walk to the new
square. A sudden frown crosses Chewbacca's face and he begins yelling
gibberish at the tiny robot. Threepio intercedes on behalf of his small
companion and begins to argue with the huge Wookiee.*

THREEPIO

He made a fair move. Screaming about it won't help you.

HAN
(*interrupting*)
Let him have it. It's not wise to upset a Wookiee.

THREEPIO

But sir, nobody worries about upsetting a droid.

HAN

That's 'cause droids don't pull people's arms out of their
sockets when they lose. Wookiees are known to do that.

THREEPIO

I see your point, sir. I suggest a new strategy, Artoo. Let the
Wookiee win.

*Luke stands in the middle of the small hold area; he seems frozen in
place. A humming lightsaber is held high over his head. Ben watches
him from the corner, studying his movements. Han watches with a bit of
smugness.*

BEN

Remember, a Jedi can feel the Force flowing through him.

LUKE

You mean it controls your actions?

BEN

Partially. But it also obeys your commands.

*Suspended at eye level, about ten feet in front of Luke, a seeker, a
chrome baseball-like robot covered with antennae, hovers slowly in a
wide arc. The ball floats to one side of the youth then to the other.
Suddenly, it makes a lightning-swift lunge and stops within a few feet of
Luke's face. Luke doesn't move and the ball backs off. It slowly moves
behind the boy, then makes another quick lunge, this time emitting a*

blood-red laser beam as it attacks. It hits Luke in the leg causing him to tumble over. Han lets loose with a burst of laughter.

> HAN
>
> Hokey religions and ancient weapons are no match for a good blaster at your side, kid.

> LUKE
>
> You don't believe in the Force, do you?

> HAN
>
> Kid, I've flown from one side of this galaxy to the other. I've seen a lot of strange stuff, but I've never seen anything to make me believe there's some all-powerful force controlling everything. There's no mystical energy field that controls my destiny.

Ben smiles quietly.

> HAN
>
> It's all a lot of simple tricks and nonsense.

> BEN
>
> I suggest you try it again, Luke.

He places a large helmet on Luke's head which covers his eyes.

> BEN
>
> This time, let go of your conscious self and act on instinct.

> LUKE
> (laughing)
> With the blast shield down, I can't even see. How am I supposed to fight?

> BEN
>
> Your eyes can deceive you. Don't trust them.

Han skeptically shakes his head as Ben throws the seeker into the air. The ball shoots straight up in the air, then drops like a rock. Luke swings the lightsaber around blindly missing the seeker, which fires off a laserbolt that hits Luke square on the seat of his pants. He lets out a pained yell and attempts to hit the seeker.

BEN

Stretch out with your feelings.

Luke stands in one place, seemingly frozen. The seeker makes a dive at Luke and, incredibly, he manages to deflect the bolt. The ball ceases firing and moves back to its original position.

BEN

You see, you can do it.

HAN

I call it luck.

BEN

In my experience, there is no such thing as luck.

HAN

Look, going good against remotes is one thing. Going good against the living? That's something else.

He notices a small light flashing on the far side of the control panel.

HAN

Looks like we're coming up to Alderaan.

He and Chewbacca head back to the cockpit.

LUKE

You know, I did feel something. I could almost see the remote.

BEN

That's good. You have taken your first step into a large world.

INT. DEATH STAR – CONFERENCE ROOM

Imperial Officer Cass stands before Governor Tarkin and the evil Dark Lord Darth Vader.

TARKIN

Yes.

OFFICER CASS

Our scout ships have reached Dantooine. They found the remains of a Rebel base, but they estimate that it has been deserted for some time. They are now conducting an extensive search of the surrounding systems.

TARKIN

She lied! She lied to us!

VADER

I told you she would never consciously betray the Rebellion.

TARKIN

Terminate her . . . immediately!

EXT. HYPERSPACE

The pirateship is just coming out of hyperspace: a strange surreal light show surrounds the ship.

INT. *MILLENNIUM FALCON* – COCKPIT

HAN

Stand by, Chewie, here we go. Cut in the sublight engines.

*He pulls back on a control lever. Outside the cockpit window stars begin
streaking past, seem to decrease in speed, then stop. Suddenly the
starship begins to shudder and violently shake about. Asteroids begin to
race towards them, battering the sides of the ship.*

                              HAN
         What the . . .? Aw, we've come out of hyperspace into a
         meteor shower. Some kind of asteroid collision. It's not on
         any of the charts.

*The giant Wookiee flips off several controls and seems very cool in the
emergency. Luke makes his way into the bouncing cockpit.*

                              LUKE
         What's going on?

                              HAN
         Our position is correct, except . . . no Alderaan!

                              LUKE
         What do you mean? Where is it?

                              HAN
         That's what I'm trying to tell you, kid. It ain't there. It's been
         totally blown away.

                              LUKE
         What? How?

*Ben moves into the cockpit behind Luke as the ship begins to settle
down.*

                              BEN
         Destroyed . . . by the Empire!

                              HAN
         The entire starfleet couldn't destroy the whole planet. It'd
         take a thousand ships with more fire power than I've . . .

*A signal light starts flashing on the control panel and a muffled alarm
starts humming.*

                              HAN
         There's another ship coming in.

LUKE

Maybe they know what happened.

BEN

It's an Imperial fighter.

Chewbacca barks his concern. A huge explosion bursts outside the cockpit window, shaking the ship violently. A tiny, finned Imperial TIE fighter races past the cockpit window.

LUKE

It followed us!

BEN

No. It's a short range fighter.

HAN

There aren't any bases around here. Where did it come from?

EXT. SPACE

The fighter races past the Corellian pirateship.

INT. *MILLENNIUM FALCON* – COCKPIT

LUKE

It sure is leaving in a big hurry. If they identify us, we're in big trouble.

HAN

Not if I can help it. Chewie . . . jam its transmissions.

BEN

It'd be as well to let it go. It's too far out of range.

HAN

Not for long . . .

EXT. SPACE

The pirateship zooms over the camera and away into the vastness of space after the Imperial TIE fighter.

INT. *MILLENNIUM FALCON* – COCKPIT

The tension mounts as the pirateship gains on the tiny fighter. In the distance, one of the stars becomes brighter until it is obvious that the TIE ship is heading for it. Ben stands behind Chewbacca.

> BEN
>
> A fighter that size couldn't get this deep into space on its own.

> LUKE
>
> Then he must have gotten lost, been part of a convoy, or something . . .

> HAN
>
> Well, he ain't going to be around long enough to tell anyone about us.

EXT. SPACE

The TIE fighter is losing ground to the larger pirateship as they race towards camera and disappear overhead.

INT. *MILLENNIUM FALCON* – COCKPIT

The distant star can now be distinguished as a small moon or planet.

> LUKE
>
> Look at him. He's heading for that small moon.

> HAN
>
> I think I can get him before he gets there . . . he's almost in range.

The small moon opens to take on the appearance of a monstrous spherical battle station.

> BEN
>
> That's not a moon! It's a space station.

> HAN
>
> It's too big to be a space station.

> LUKE
>
> I have a very bad feeling about this.

                              BEN
Turn the ship around!

                              HAN
Yeah. I think you're right. Full reverse! Chewie, lock in the
auxiliary power.

*The pirateship shudders and the TIE fighter accelerates away towards
the gargantuan battle station.*

                              LUKE
Why are we still moving towards it?

                              HAN
We're caught in a tractor beam! It's pulling us in.

                              LUKE
But there's gotta be something you can do!

                              HAN
There's nothin' I can do about it, kid. I'm in full power. I'm
going to have to shut down. But they're not going to get me
without a fight!

Ben Kenobi puts a hand on his shoulder.

                              BEN
You can't win. But there are alternatives to fighting.

INT. *MILLENNIUM FALCON* – DEATH STAR

*As the battered starship is towed closer to the awesome metal moon, the
immense size of the massive battle station becomes staggering. Running
along the equator of the gigantic sphere is a mile-high band of huge
docking ports into which the helpless pirateship is dragged.*

EXT. DEATH STAR – HUGE PORT DOORS

The helpless Millennium Falcon *is pulled past a docking port control
room and huge laser turret cannons.*

            VOICE OVER DEATH STAR INTERCOM
Clear Bay twenty-three-seven. We are opening the magnetic
field.

INT. DEATH STAR – DOCKING BAY 2037

The pirateship is pulled in through port doors of the Death Star, coming to rest in a huge hangar. Thirty stormtroopers stand at attention in a central assembly area.

> OFFICER
>
> To your stations!

> OFFICER
> (*to another officer*)
>
> Come with me.

INT. DEATH STAR – HALLWAY

Stormtroopers run to their posts.

INT. DEATH STAR – HANGAR 2037

A line of stormtroopers marches towards the pirateship in readiness to board it, while other troopers stand with weapons ready to fire.

> OFFICER
>
> Close all outboard shields! Close all outboard shields!

INT. DEATH STAR – CONFERENCE ROOM

Tarkin pushes a button and responds to intercom buzz.

> TARKIN
>
> Yes.

> VOICE
> (*over intercom*)
>
> We've captured a freighter entering the remains of the Alderaan system. Its markings match those of a ship that blasted its way out of Mos Eisley.

> VADER
>
> They must be trying to return the stolen plans to the princess. She may yet be of some use to us.

INT. DEATH STAR – DOCKING BAY 2037

Vader and a commander approach the troops as an Officer and several heavily armed troops exit the spacecraft.

> VOICE
> (*over intercom*)
> Unlock one-five-seven and nine. Release charges.

> OFFICER
> (*to Vader*)
> There's no one on board, sir. According to the log, the crew abandoned ship right after takeoff. It must be a decoy, sir. Several of the escape pods have been jettisoned.

> VADER
> Did you find any droids?

> OFFICER
> No, sir. If there were any on board, they must also have jettisoned.

> VADER
> Send a scanning crew on board. I want every part of this ship checked.

> OFFICER
> Yes, sir.

> VADER
> I sense something . . . a presence I haven't felt since . . .

Vader turns quickly and exits the hangar.

> OFFICER
> Get me a scanning crew in here on the double. I want every part of this ship checked!

INT. *MILLENNIUM FALCON* – HALLWAY

A trooper runs through the hallway heading for the exit. In a few moments all is quiet. The muffled sounds of a distant officer giving orders finally fade. Two floor panels suddenly pop up, revealing Han Solo and Luke. Ben Kenobi sticks his head out of a third locker.

LUKE

Boy, it's lucky you had these compartments.

HAN

I use them for smuggling. I never thought I'd be smuggling myself in them. This is ridiculous. Even if I could take off, I'd never get past the tractor beam.

BEN

Leave that to me!

HAN

Damn fool. I knew that you were going to say that!

BEN

Who's the more foolish . . . the fool or the fool who follows him?

Han shakes his head, muttering to himself. Chewbacca agrees.

INT. DEATH STAR – MAIN FORWARD BAY

Two crewmen carry a heavy box on board the ship, past two stormtroopers guarding either side of the ramp.

TROOPER

The ship's all yours. If the scanners pick up anything, report it immediately. All right, let's go.

The crewmen enter the pirateship and a loud crashing sound is followed by a voice calling to the guard below.

HAN

Hey down there, could you give us a hand with this?

The stormtroopers enter the ship and a quick round of gunfire is heard.

INT. DEATH STAR – FORWARD BAY – COMMAND OFFICE

In a very small command office near the entrance to the pirateship, a Gantry Officer looks out his window and notices the guards are missing. He speaks into the comlink.

GANTRY OFFICER

TX-four-two-one. Why aren't you at your post? TX-four-two-one, do you copy?

A stormtrooper comes down the ramp of the pirateship and waves to the gantry officer, pointing to his ear, indicating his comlink is not working. The gantry officer shakes his head in disgust and heads for the door, giving his aide an annoyed look.

GANTRY OFFICER

Take over. We've got a bad transmitter. I'll see what I can do.

As the officer approaches the door, it slides open revealing the towering Chewbacca. The gantry officer, in a momentary state of shock, stumbles backward. With a bone-chilling howl, the giant Wookiee flattens the officer with one blow. The aide immediately reaches for his pistol, but is blasted by Han, dressed as an Imperial stormtrooper.

Ben and the robots enter the room, quickly followed by Luke, also dressed as a stormtrooper. Luke quickly removes his helmet.

LUKE

You know, between his howling and your blasting everything in sight, it's a wonder the whole station doesn't know we're here.

HAN

Bring them on! I prefer a straight fight to all this sneaking around.

THREEPIO

We found the computer outlet, sir.

Ben feeds some information into the computer and a map of the city appears on the monitor. He begins to inspect it carefully. Threepio and Artoo look over the control panel. Artoo finds something that makes him whistle wildly.

BEN

Plug in. He should be able to interpret the entire Imperial computer network.

Artoo punches his claw arm into the computer socket and the vast Imperial brain network comes to life, feeding information to the little robot. After a few moments, he beeps something.

THREEPIO

He says he's found the main control to the power beam that's holding the ship here. He'll try to make the precise location appear on the monitor.

The computer monitor flashes readouts.

THREEPIO

The tractor beam is coupled to the main reactor in seven locations. A power loss at one of the terminals will allow the ship to leave.

Ben studies the data on the monitor readout.

BEN

I don't think you boys can help. I must go alone.

HAN

Whatever you say. I've done more than I bargained for on this trip already.

LUKE

I want to go with you.

BEN

Be patient, Luke. Stay and watch over the droids.

LUKE

But he can . . .

BEN

They must be delivered safely or other star systems will suffer the same fate as Alderaan. Your destiny lies along a different path from mine. The Force will be with you . . . always!

Ben adjusts the lightsaber on his belt and silently steps out of the command office, then disappears down a long gray hallway. Chewbacca barks a comment and Han shakes his head in agreement.

HAN

Boy, you said it, Chewie.

Han looks at Luke.

HAN

Where did you dig up that old fossil?

LUKE

Ben is a great man.

HAN

Yeah, great at getting us into trouble.

LUKE

I didn't hear you give any ideas . . .

HAN

Well, anything would be better than just hanging around
waiting for them to pick us up . . .

LUKE

Who do you think . . .

*Suddenly Artoo begins to whistle and beep a blue streak. Luke goes over
to him.*

LUKE

What is it?

THREEPIO

I'm afraid I'm not quite sure, sir. He says, 'I found her,' and
keeps repeating, 'She's here.'

LUKE

Well, who . . . who has he found?

Artoo whistles a frantic reply.

THREEPIO

Princess Leia.

LUKE

The princess? She's here?

HAN

Princess?

LUKE

Where . . . where is she?

HAN

Princess? What's going on?

THREEPIO

Level five, detention block AA-twenty-three. I'm afraid she's
scheduled to be terminated.

LUKE

Oh, no! We've got to do something.

HAN

What are you talking about?

LUKE

The droid belongs to her. She's the one in the message.
We've got to help her.

HAN

Now, look, don't get any funny ideas. The old man wants us
to wait right here.

LUKE

But he didn't know she was here. Look, will you just find a
way back into that detention block?

HAN

I'm not going anywhere.

LUKE

They're going to execute her. Look, a few minutes ago you
said you didn't want to just wait here to be captured. Now all
you want to do is stay.

HAN

Marching into the detention area is not what I had in mind.

LUKE

But they're going to kill her!

HAN

Better her than me.

LUKE

She's rich.

Chewbacca growls.

HAN

Rich?

LUKE

Yes. Rich, powerful! Listen, if you were to rescue her, the reward would be . . .

HAN

What?

LUKE

Well, more wealth than you can imagine.

HAN

I don't know, I can imagine quite a bit!

LUKE

You'll get it!

HAN

I'd better!

LUKE

You will . . .

HAN

All right, kid. But you'd better be right about this!

He looks at Chewie, who grunts a short grunt.

LUKE

All right.

HAN

What's your plan?

LUKE

Uh . . . Threepio, hand me those binders there, will you?

He moves towards Chewbacca with electronic cuffs.

LUKE

Okay. Now, I'm going to put these on you.

Chewie lets out a hideous growl.

LUKE

Okay, Han, you put these on.

He sheepishly hands the binders to Han.

HAN

Don't worry, Chewie. I think I know what he has in mind.

The Wookiee has a worried and frightened look on his face as Han binds him with electronic cuffs.

THREEPIO

Master Luke, sir! Pardon me for asking . . . but, ah . . . what should Artoo and I do if we're discovered here?

LUKE

Lock the door!

HAN

And hope they don't have blasters.

THREEPIO

That isn't very reassuring.

Luke and Han put on their armored stormtrooper helmets and start off into the giant Imperial Death Star.

INT. DEATH STAR – DETENTION AREA – ELEVATOR TUBE

Han and Luke try to look inconspicuous in their armored suits as they wait for a vacuum elevator to arrive. Troops, bureaucrats, and robots bustle about, ignoring the trio completely. Only a few give the giant Wookiee a curious glance.

Finally a small elevator arrives and the trio enters.

LUKE

I can't see a thing in this helmet.

A bureaucrat races to get aboard also, but is signaled away by Han. The door to the pod-like vehicle slides closed and the elevator car takes off through a vacuum tube.

INT. DEATH STAR – MAIN HALLWAY

Several Imperial officers walk through the wide main passageway. They pass several stormtroopers and a robot similar to Threepio but with an insect face. At the far end of the hallway, a passing flash of Ben Kenobi appears, then disappears down a small hallway. His appearance is so fleeting that it is hard to tell if he is real or just an illusion. No one in the hallway seems to notice him.

INT. DEATH STAR – ELEVATOR – DETENTION AREA

Luke and Han step forward to exit the elevator, but the door slides open behind them. The giant Wookiee and his two guards enter the old gray security station. Guards and laser gates are everywhere. Han whispers to Luke under his breath.

> HAN
>
> This is not going to work.

> LUKE
>
> Why didn't you say so before?

> HAN
>
> I did say so before!

INT. DETENTION AREA

Elevator doors open. A tall, grim-looking Officer approaches the trio.

> OFFICER
>
> Where are you taking this . . . thing?

Chewie growls a bit at the remark but Han nudges him to shut up.

> LUKE
>
> Prisoner transfer from Block one-one-three-eight.

> OFFICER
>
> I wasn't notified. I'll have to clear it.

The officer goes back to his console and begins to punch in the information. There are only three other troopers in the area. Luke and Han survey the situation, checking all of the alarms, laser gates, and camera eyes. Han unfastens one of Chewbacca's electronic cuffs and shrugs to Luke.

Suddenly, Chewbacca throws up his hands and lets out with one of his ear-piercing howls. He grabs Han's laser rifle.

> HAN
>
> Look out! He's loose!

LUKE

He's going to pull us apart!

HAN

Go get him!

*The startled guards are momentarily dumbfounded. Luke and Han
have already pulled out their laser pistols and are blasting away at the
terrifying Wookiee. Their barrage of laserfire misses Chewbacca, but hits
the camera eyes, laser gate controls, and the Imperial guards. The officer
is the last of the guards to fall under the laserfire just as he is about to
push the alarm system. Han rushes to the comlink system, which is
screeching questions about what is going on. He quickly checks the
computer readout.*

HAN

We've got to find out which cell this princess of yours is in.
Here it is . . . cell twenty-one-eight-seven. You go get her. I'll
hold them here.

*Luke races down one of the cell corridors. Han speaks into the buzzing
comlink.*

HAN
(*sounding official*)

Everything is under control. Situation normal.

INTERCOM VOICE

What happened?

HAN
(*getting nervous*)

Uh . . . had a slight weapons malfunction. But, uh,
everything's perfectly all right now. We're fine. We're all fine
here, now, thank you. How are you?

INTERCOM VOICE

We're sending a squad up.

HAN

Uh, uh, negative, negative. We had a reactor leak here now.
Give us a few minutes to lock it down. Large leak . . . very
dangerous.

Who is this? What's your operating number?

Han blasts the comlink and it explodes.

HAN

Boring conversation anyway.
(*yelling down the hall*)
Luke! We're going to have company!

INT. DEATH STAR — CELL ROW

Luke stops in front of one of the cells and blasts the door away with his laser pistol. When the smoke clears, Luke sees the dazzling young princess-senator. She had been sleeping and is now looking at him with an uncomprehending look on her face. Luke is stunned by her incredible beauty and stands staring at her with his mouth hanging open.

LEIA
(*finally*)
Aren't you a little short for a stormtrooper?

Luke takes off his helmet, coming out of it.

LUKE

What? Oh . . . the uniform. I'm Luke Skywalker. I'm here to rescue you.

LEIA

You're who?

LUKE

I'm here to rescue you. I've got your R2 unit. I'm here with Ben Kenobi.

LEIA

Ben Kenobi is here! Where is he?

LUKE

Come on!

INT. DEATH STAR — CONFERENCE ROOM

Darth Vader paces the room as Governor Tarkin sits at the far end of the conference table.

VADER

He is here . . .

TARKIN

Obi-Wan Kenobi! What makes you think so?

VADER

A tremor in the Force. The last time I felt it was in the presence of my old master.

TARKIN

Surely he must be dead by now.

VADER

Don't underestimate the Force.

TARKIN

The Jedi are extinct, their fire has gone out of the universe. You, my friend, are all that's left of their religion.

There is a quiet buzz on the comlink.

TARKIN

Yes.

INTERCOM VOICE

Governor Tarkin, we have an emergency alert in detention block AA-twenty-three.

TARKIN

The princess! Put all sections on alert!

VADER

Obi-Wan is here. The Force is with him.

TARKIN

If you're right, he must not be allowed to escape.

VADER

Escape may not be his plan. I must face him alone.

INT. DEATH STAR – DETENTION AREA – HALLWAY

An ominous buzzing sound is heard on the other side of the elevator door.

HAN

Chewie!

Chewbacca responds with a growling noise.

HAN

Get behind me! Get behind me!

A series of explosions knocks a hole in the elevator door through which several Imperial troops begin to emerge.

Han and Chewie fire their laser pistols at them through the smoke and flames. They turn and run down the cell hallway, meeting up with Luke and Leia rushing towards them.

Can't get out that way.

LEIA

Looks like you managed to cut off our only escape route.

HAN
(*sarcastically*)

Maybe you'd like it back in your cell, Your Highness.

Luke takes a small comlink transmitter from his belt as they continue to exchange fire with stormtroopers making their way down the corridor.

LUKE

See-Threepio! See-Threepio!

THREEPIO
(*over comlink*)

Yes, sir?

LUKE

We've been cut off! Are there any other ways out of the cell
bay? . . . What was that? I didn't copy!

INT. DEATH STAR – MAIN BAY GANTRY – CONTROL TOWER

*Threepio paces the control center as little Artoo beeps and whistles a blue
streak. Threepio yells into the small comlink transmitter.*

THREEPIO

I said, all systems have been alerted to your presence, sir. The
main entrance seems to be the only way out; all other
information on your level is restricted.

Someone begins banging on the door.

TROOPER VOICE

Open up in there!

THREEPIO

Oh, no!

INT. DEATH STAR – DETENTION AREA – CORRIDOR

*Luke and Leia crouch together in an alcove for protection as they
continue to exchange fire with troops. Han and Chewbacca are barely
able to keep the stormtroopers at bay at the far end of the hallway. The
laserfire is very intense, and smoke fills the narrow cell corridor.*

LUKE

There isn't any other way out.

HAN

I can't hold them off for ever! Now what?

LEIA

This is some rescue. When you came in here, didn't you have
a plan for getting out?

HAN
(*pointing to Luke*)
He is the brains, sweetheart.

Luke manages a sheepish grin and shrugs his shoulders.

LUKE

Well, I didn't . . .

*The princess grabs Luke's gun and fires at a small grate in the wall next
to Han, almost frying him.*

HAN

What the hell are you doing?

LEIA

Somebody has to save our skins. Into the garbage chute, wise
guy.

*She jumps through the narrow opening as Han and Chewbacca look on
in amazement. Chewbacca sniffs the garbage chute and says something.*

HAN

Get in there you big furry oaf! I don't care what you smell!
Get in there and don't worry about it.

*Han gives him a big kick and the Wookiee disappears into the tiny
opening. Luke and Han continue firing as they work their way towards
the opening.*

HAN

Wonderful girl! Either I'm going to kill her or I'm beginning
to like her. Get in there!

*Luke ducks laserfire as he jumps into the darkness. Han fires off a
couple of quick blasts creating a smoky cover, then slides into the chute
himself and is gone.*

INT. DEATH STAR – GARBAGE ROOM

Han tumbles into a large room filled with garbage and muck. Luke is

already stumbling around looking for an exit. He finds a small
hatchway and struggles to get it open. It won't budge.

HAN
(*sarcastically*)
Oh! The garbage chute was a really wonderful idea. What an
incredible smell you've discovered! Let's get out of here! Get
away from there . . .

LUKE
No! Wait!

Han draws his laser pistol and fires at the hatch. The laserbolt ricochets
wildly around the small metal room. Everyone dives for cover in the
garbage as the bolt explodes almost on top of them. Leia climbs out of
the garbage with a rather grim look on her face.

LUKE
Will you forget it? I already tried it. It's magnetically sealed.

LEIA
Put that thing away! You're going to get us all killed.

HAN
Absolutely, Your Worship. Look, I had everything under
control until you led us down here. You know, it's not going
to take them long to figure out what happened to us.

LEIA
It could be worse.

A loud, horrible, unhuman moan works its way up from the murky
depths. Chewbacca lets out a terrified howl and begins to back away.
Han and Luke stand fast with their laser pistols drawn. The Wookiee is
cowering near one of the walls.

HAN
It's worse.

LUKE
There's something alive in here!

HAN
That's your imagination.

LUKE

Something just moved past my leg! Look! Did you see that?

HAN

What?

LUKE

Help!

Suddenly, Luke is yanked under the garbage.

HAN

Luke! Luke! Luke!

He tries to get to Luke. Luke surfaces with a gasp of air and thrashing of limbs. A membrane tentacle is wrapped around his throat.

LEIA

Luke!

She extends a long pipe towards him.

LEIA

Luke, Luke, grab a hold of this.

LUKE

Blast it, will you! My gun's jammed.

HAN

Where?

LUKE

Anywhere! Oh!!

Solo fires his gun downward. Luke is pulled back into the muck by the slimy tentacle.

HAN

Luke! Luke!

Suddenly, the walls of the garbage receptacle shudder and move in a couple of inches. Then everything is deathly quiet. Han and Leia give each other a worried look as Chewbacca howls in the corner. With a rush of bubbles and muck, Luke suddenly bobs to the surface.

LEIA

Grab him!

Luke seems to be released by the thing.

LEIA

What happened?

LUKE

I don't know, it just let go of me and disappeared . . .

HAN

I've got a very bad feeling about this.

Before anyone can say anything the walls begin to rumble and edge towards the Rebels.

LUKE

The walls are moving!

LEIA

Don't just stand there. Try and brace it with something.

They place poles and long metal beams between the closing walls, but they are simply snapped and bent as the giant trashmasher rumbles on. The situation doesn't look too good.

LUKE

Wait a minute!

He pulls out his comlink.

LUKE

Threepio! Come in, Threepio! Threepio! Where could he be?

INT. DEATH STAR – MAIN GANTRY – COMMAND OFFICE

A soft buzzer and the muted voice of Luke calling out to See-Threepio can be heard on Threepio's hand comlink, which is sitting on the deserted computer console. Artoo and Threepio are nowhere in sight. Suddenly, there is a great explosion and the door of the control tower flies across the floor. Four armed stormtroopers enter the chamber.

FIRST TROOPER

Take over!

> (*pointing to a dead officer*)

See to him! Look there!

A trooper pushes a button and the supply cabinet door slides open. See-Threepio and Artoo-Detoo are inside. Artoo follows his bronze companion out into the office.

THREEPIO

They're madmen! They're heading for the prison level. If you hurry, you might catch them.

FIRST OFFICER
(to his troops)

Follow me! You stand guard.

The troops hustle off down the hallway, leaving a Guard to watch over the command office.

THREEPIO
(to Artoo)

Come on!

The guard aims a blaster at them.

THREEPIO

Oh! All this excitement has overrun the circuits in my counterpart here. If you don't mind, I'd like to take him down to maintenance.

GUARD

All right.

The guard nods and Threepio, with little Artoo in tow, hurries out the door.

INT. DEATH STAR — GARBAGE ROOM

As the walls rumble closed, the room gets smaller and smaller. Chewie is whining and trying to hold a wall back with his giant paws. Han is leaning back against the other wall. Garbage is snapping and popping. Luke is trying to reach Threepio.

LUKE

Threepio! Come in. Threepio! Threepio!

Han and Leia try to brace the contracting walls with a pole. Leia begins to sink into the trash.

HAN

Get to the top!

LEIA

I can't.

LUKE

Where would he be? Threepio! Threepio, will you come in?

INT. DEATH STAR — MAIN FORWARD BAY — SERVICE PANEL

THREEPIO

They aren't here! Something must have happened to them.
See if they've been captured.

*Little Artoo carefully plugs his claw arm into a new wall socket and a
complex array of electronic sounds spew from the tiny robot.*

THREEPIO

Hurry!

INT. DEATH STAR — GARBAGE ROOM

*The walls are only feet apart. Leia and Han are braced against the
walls. The princess is frightened. They look at each other. Leia reaches
out and takes Han's hand and holds it tightly. She's terrified and
suddenly groans as she feels the first crushing pressure against her body.*

HAN

One thing's for sure. We're all going to be a lot thinner!
(*to Leia*)
Get on top of it!

LEIA

I'm trying!

INT. DEATH STAR — MAIN FORWARD BAY — SERVICE PANEL

THREEPIO
(*to Artoo*)
Thank goodness, they haven't found them! Where could they
be?

Artoo frantically beeps something to See-Threepio.

THREEPIO

Use the comlink? Oh, my! I forgot I turned it off!

INT. DEATH STAR — GARBAGE ROOM

Meanwhile, Luke is lying on his side, trying to keep his head above the rising ooze. His comlink begins to buzz and he rips it off his belt.

INT. DEATH STAR — MAIN FORWARD BAY — SERVICE PANEL

Muffled sounds of Luke's voice over comlink can be heard, but not distinctly.

THREEPIO

Are you there, sir?

INT. DEATH STAR — GARBAGE ROOM

LUKE

Threepio!

INT. DEATH STAR — MAIN FORWARD BAY

THREEPIO

We've had some problems . . .

LUKE
(*over comlink*)

Shut down all the garbage mashers on the detention level, will you? Do you copy?

INT. DEATH STAR — GARBAGE ROOM

LUKE

Shut down all the garbage mashers on the detention level.

INT. DEATH STAR — MAIN FORWARD BAY — SERVICE PANEL

LUKE
(*over comlink*)

Shut down all the garbage mashers on the detention level.

THREEPIO
(*to Artoo*)
No. Shut them all down! Hurry!

Threepio holds his head in agony as he hears the incredible screaming and hollering from Luke's comlink.

THREEPIO
Listen to them! They're dying, Artoo! Curse my metal body! I wasn't fast enough. It's all my fault! My poor master!

LUKE
(*over comlink*)
Threepio, we're all right!

INT. DEATH STAR – GARBAGE ROOM

The screaming and hollering is the sound of joyous relief. The walls have stopped moving. Han, Chewie and Leia embrace in the background.

LUKE
We're all right. You did great.

He moves to the pressure-sensitive hatch, looking for a number.

LUKE
Hey . . . hey, open the pressure maintenance hatch on unit number . . . where are we?

INT. DEATH STAR – MAIN FORWARD BAY – SERVICE PANEL

Threepio looks at the computer panel as Han reads the number

HAN
(*over comlink*)
Three-two-six-eight-two-seven.

INT. DEATH STAR – TRACTOR BEAM – POWER GENERATOR TRENCH

Ben enters a humming service trench that powers the huge tractor beam. The trench seems to be a hundred miles deep. The clacking sound of huge switching devices can be heard. The old Jedi edges his way along a narrow ledge leading to a control panel that connects two large cables.

He carefully makes several adjustments in the computer terminal, and several lights on the board go from red to blue.

INT. DEATH STAR — UNUSED HALLWAY

The group exits the garbage room into a dusty, unused hallway. Han and Leia remove the trooper suits and strap on the blaster belts.

HAN

If we can just avoid any more female advice, we ought to be able to get out of here.

Luke smiles and scratches his head as he takes a blaster from Solo.

LUKE

Well, let's get moving!

Chewie begins growling and points to the hatch to the garbage room as he runs away and then stops howling.

HAN
(to Chewie)

Where are you going?

The dianoga bangs against the hatch and a long, slimy tentacle works its way out of the doorway searching for a victim. Han aims his pistol.

LEIA

No, wait. They'll hear!

Han fires at the doorway. The noise of the blast echoes relentlessly throughout the empty passageway. Luke simply shakes his head in disgust.

HAN
(to Chewie)

Come here, you big coward!

Chewie shakes his head 'no.'

HAN

Chewie! Come here!

LEIA

Listen. I don't know who you are, or where you come from, but from now on, you do as I tell you. Okay?

Han is stunned at the command of the petite young girl.

HAN

Look, Your Worshipfulness, let's get one thing straight! I take orders from one person! Me!

LEIA

It's a wonder you're still alive.
(looking at Chewie)
Will somebody get this big walking carpet out of my way?

Han watches her start away. He looks at Luke.

HAN

No reward is worth this.

They follow her, moving swiftly down the deserted corridor.

INT. DEATH STAR — POWER TRENCH

Suddenly, a door behind Ben slides open and a detachment of stormtroopers marches to the power trench. Ben instantly slips into the shadows as an Officer moves to within a few feet of him.

OFFICER

Secure this entry area until the alert is cancelled.

FIRST TROOPER

Give me regular reports.

All but two of the stormtroopers leave.

FIRST TROOPER

Do you know what's going on?

SECOND TROOPER

Maybe it's another drill.

Ben moves around the tractor beam, watching the stormtroopers as they turn their backs to him. Ben gestures with his hand towards them, as the troops think they hear something in the other hallway. With the help of the Force, Ben deftly slips past the troopers and into the main hallway.

What was that?

FIRST TROOPER

Oh, it's nothing. Don't worry about it.

INT. DEATH STAR – HALLWAY

Luke, Han, Chewbacca, and Leia run down an empty hallway and stop before a bay window overlooking the pirateship. Troopers are milling around the ship. Luke takes out his pocket comlink.

> HAN
> (*looking at his ship*)

There she is.

> LUKE

See-Threepio, do you copy?

> THREEPIO
> (*over comlink*)

For the moment. Uh, we're in the main hangar across from the ship.

> LUKE

We're right above you. Stand by.

Han is watching the dozen or so troops moving in and out of the pirateship. Leia moves towards Han, touches his arm, and points out the window to the ship.

> LEIA

You came in that thing? You're braver than I thought.

> HAN

Nice! Come on!

He gives her a dirty look, and they start off down the hallway. They round a corner and run right into twenty Imperial stormtroopers heading towards them. Both groups are taken by surprise and stop in their tracks.

> FIRST TROOPER

It's them! Blast them!

Before even thinking, Han draws his laser pistol and charges the troops, firing. His blast knocks one of the stormtroopers into the air. Chewie follows his captain down the corridor, stepping over the fallen trooper on the floor.

(*to Luke and Leia*)

Get back to the ship!

LUKE

Where are you going? Come back!

Han has already rounded a corner and does not hear.

LEIA

He certainly has courage.

LUKE

What good will it do us if he gets himself killed? Come on!

Luke is furious but doesn't have time to think about it for muted alarms begin to go off down on the hangar deck. Luke and Leia start off towards the starship hangar.

INT. DEATH STAR — SUBHALLWAY

Han chases the stormtroopers down a long subhallway. He is yelling and brandishing his laser pistol. The troops reach a dead end and are forced to turn and fight. Han stops a few feet from them and assumes a defensive position. The troops begin to raise their laser guns. Soon all the troopers are moving into an attack position in front of the lone starpirate. Han's determined look begins to fade as the troops begin to advance. Solo jumps backward as they fire at him.

INT. DEATH STAR — SUBHALLWAY

Chewbacca runs down the subhallway in a last-ditch attempt to save his bold captain. Suddenly, he hears the firing of laser guns and yelling. Around the corner shoots Han, pirate extraordinaire, running for his life, followed by a host of furious stormtroopers. Chewbacca turns and starts running the other way also.

INT. DEATH STAR — HALLWAY

Luke fires his laser pistol wildly as he and Leia rush down a narrow subhallway, chased by several stormtroopers. They quickly reach the end of the subhallway and race through an open hatchway.

INT. DEATH STAR – CENTRAL CORE SHAFT

Luke and Leia race through the hatch on to a narrow bridge that spans a huge, deep shaft that seems to go into infinity. The bridge has been retracted into the wall of the shaft, and Luke almost rushes into the abyss. He loses his balance off the end of the bridge as Leia, behind him, takes hold of his arm and pulls him back.

> LUKE
> *(gasping)*
> I think we took a wrong turn.

Blasts from the stormtroopers' laser guns explode near by, reminding them of the oncoming danger. Luke fires back at the advancing troops. Leia reaches over and hits a switch that pops the hatch door shut with a resounding boom, leaving them precariously perched on a short piece of bridge overhang. Laserfire from the troopers continues to hit the steel door.

> LEIA
> There's no lock!

Luke blasts the controls with his laser pistol.

> LUKE
> That oughta hold it for a while.

> LEIA
> Quick, we've got to get across. Find the control that extends the bridge.

> LUKE
> Oh, I think I just blasted it.

He looks at the blasted bridge control while the stormtroopers on the opposite side of the door begin making ominous drilling and pounding sounds.

> LEIA
> They're coming through!

Luke notices something on his stormtrooper belt, when laserfire hits the wall behind him. Luke aims his laser pistol at a stormtrooper perched on a higher bridge overhang across the abyss from them. They exchange

*fire. Two more troopers appear on another overhang, also firing. A
trooper is hit, and grabs at his chest.*

*Another trooper standing on a bridge overhang is hit by Luke's laserfire,
and plummets down the shaft. Troopers move back off the bridge; Luke
hands his gun to Leia.*

LUKE

Here, hold this.

*Luke pulls a thin nylon cable from his trooper utility belt. It has a
grappler hook on it.*

*A trooper appears on a bridge overhang and fires at Luke and Leia. As
Luke works with the rope, Leia returns the laser volley. Another trooper
appears and fires at them, as Leia returns his fire as well. Suddenly, the
hatch door begins to open, revealing the feet of more troops.*

LEIA

Here they come!

*Leia hits one of the stormtroopers on the bridge above, and he falls into
the abyss. Luke tosses the rope across the gorge and it wraps itself
around an outcropping of pipes. He tugs on the rope to make sure it is*

secure, then grabs the princess in his arms. Leia looks at Luke, then kisses him quickly on the lips. Luke is very surprised.

LEIA

For luck!

Luke pushes off and they swing across the treacherous abyss to the corresponding hatchway on the opposite side. Just as Luke and Leia reach the far side of the canyon, the stormtroopers break through the hatch and begin to fire at the escaping duo. Luke returns the fire before ducking into the tiny subhallway.

INT. DEATH STAR — NARROW PASSAGEWAY

Ben hides in the shadows of a narrow passageway as several stormtroopers rush past him in the main hallway. He checks to make sure they're gone, then runs down the hallway in the opposite direction. Darth Vader appears at the far end of the hallway and starts after the old Jedi.

INT. DEATH STAR — MAIN FORWARD BAY

Threepio looks around at the troops milling about the pirateship entry ramp.

THREEPIO

Where could they be?

Artoo, plugged into the computer socket, turns his dome left and right, beeping a response.

INT. DEATH STAR — CORRIDOR — BLAST SHIELD DOOR

Han and Chewbacca run down a long corridor with several troopers hot on their trail.

TROOPER

Close the blast doors!

At the end of the hallway, blast doors begin to close in front of them. The young starpilot and his furry companion race past the huge doors just as they are closing, and manage to get off a couple of laserblasts at the pursuing troops before the doors slam shut.

Open the blast doors! Open the blast doors!

INT. DEATH STAR — HALLWAY LEADING TO MAIN FORWARD BAY

Ben hurries along one of the tunnels leading to the hangar where the pirateship waits. Just before he reaches the hangar, Darth Vader steps into view at the end of the tunnel, not ten feet away. Vader lights his saber. Ben also ignites his and steps slowly forward.

VADER

I've been waiting for you, Obi-Wan. We meet again, at last. The circle is now complete.

Ben Kenobi moves with elegant ease into a classical offensive position. The fearsome Dark Knight takes a defensive stance.

VADER

When I left you, I was but the learner; now I am the master.

BEN

Only a master of evil, Darth.

The two Galactic warriors stand perfectly still for a few moments, sizing each other up and waiting for the right moment. Ben seems to be under increasing pressure and strain, as if an invisible weight were being placed upon him. He shakes his head and, blinking, tries to clear his head.

Ben makes a sudden lunge at the huge warrior but is checked by a lightning movement of The Sith. A masterful slash stroke by Vader is blocked by the old Jedi. Another of the Jedi's blows is blocked, then countered. Ben moves around the Dark Lord and starts backing into the massive starship hangar. The two powerful warriors stand motionless for a few moments with laser swords locked in mid-air, creating a low buzzing sound.

VADER

Your powers are weak, old man.

BEN

You can't win, Darth. If you strike me down I shall become more powerful than you can possibly imagine.

Their lightsabers continue to meet in combat.

INT. DEATH STAR — MAIN FORWARD BAY

Han Solo and Chewbacca, their weapons in hand, lean back against the wall, surveying the forward bay, watching the Imperial stormtroopers make their rounds in the hangar.

> HAN
> Didn't we just leave this party?

Chewbacca growls a reply, as Luke and the princess join them.

> HAN
> What kept you?

> LEIA
> We ran into some old friends.

> LUKE
> Is the ship all right?

> HAN
> Seems okay, if we can get to it: Just hope the old man got the tractor beam out of commission.

INT. DEATH STAR — HALLWAY

Vader and Ben Kenobi continue their powerful duel. As they hit their lightsabers together, lightning flashes on impact. Troopers look on in interest as the old Jedi and Dark Lord of the Sith fight. Suddenly, Luke spots the battle from his group's vantage point.

> LUKE
> Look!

Luke, Leia, Han, and Chewie look up and see Ben and Vader emerging from the hallways on the far side of the docking bay.

INT. DEATH STAR — DOCKING BAY

Threepio and Artoo-Detoo are in the center of the Death Star's Imperial docking bay.

> THREEPIO
> Come on, Artoo, we're going!

He ducks out of sight as the seven stormtroopers who were guarding the starship rush past them heading towards Ben and Vader. He pulls on Artoo.

INT. DEATH STAR — HALLWAY

Solo, Chewie, Luke, and Leia tensely watch the duel. The troops rush towards the battling knights.

> HAN
>
> Now's our chance! Go!

They start for the Millennium Falcon.

Ben sees the troops charging towards him and realizes that he is trapped. Vader takes advantage of Ben's momentary distraction and brings his mighty lightsaber down on the old man. Ben manages to deflect the blow and swiftly turns around.

The old Jedi Knight looks over his shoulder at Luke, lifts his sword from Vader's, then watches his opponent with a serene look on his face.

Vader brings his sword down, cutting old Ben in half. Ben's cloak falls to the floor in two parts, but Ben is not in it. Vader is puzzled at Ben's disappearance and pokes at the empty cloak. As the guards are distracted the adventurers and the robots reach the starship.

Luke sees Ben cut in two and starts for him. Aghast, he yells out.

> LUKE
>
> No!

The stormtroopers turn towards Luke and begin firing at him. The robots are already moving up the ramp into the Millennium Falcon, *while Luke, transfixed by anger and awe, returns their fire. Solo joins in the laserfire. Vader looks up and advances towards them, as one of his troopers is struck down.*

> HAN
> (*to Luke*)
>
> Come on!

> LEIA
>
> Come on! Luke, it's too late!

Blast the door! Kid!

Luke fires his laser pistol at the door control panel, and it explodes. The doors begin to slide shut. Three troopers charge forward firing laserbolts, as the door slides to a close behind them . . . shutting Vader and the other troops out of the docking bay. A stormtrooper lies dead at the feet of his onrushing compatriots. Luke starts for the advancing troops, as Solo and Leia move up the ramp into the pirateship. He fires, hitting a stormtrooper, who crumples to the floor.

BEN'S VOICE
Run, Luke! Run!

Luke looks around to see where the voice came from. He turns towards the pirateship, ducking Imperial gunfire from the troopers, and races into the ship.

INT. *MILLENNIUM FALCON* – COCKPIT

Han pulls back on the controls and the ship begins to move. The dull thud of laserbolts can be heard bouncing off the outside of the ship as Chewie adjusts his controls.

HAN
I hope the old man got that tractor beam out of commission, or this is going to be a real short trip. Okay, hit it!

Chewbacca growls in agreement.

EXT. *MILLENNIUM FALCON*

The Millennium Falcon *powers away from the Death Star docking bay, makes a spectacular turn and disappears into the vastness of space.*

INT. *MILLENNIUM FALCON* – CENTRAL HOLD AREA

Luke, saddened by the loss of Obi-Wan Kenobi, stares off blankly as the robots look on. Leia puts a blanket around him protectively, and Luke turns and looks up at her. She sits down beside him.

INT. *MILLENNIUM FALCON* – COCKPIT

Solo spots approaching enemy ships.

> HAN
> (*to Chewie*)
> We're coming up on their sentry ships. Hold 'em off! Angle the deflector shields while I charge up with the main guns!

INT. *MILLENNIUM FALCON* – CENTRAL HOLD AREA

Luke looks downward sadly, shaking his head back and forth, as the princess smiles comfortingly at him.

> LUKE
> I can't believe he's gone.

Artoo-Detoo beeps a reply.

> LEIA
> There wasn't anything you could have done.

Han rushes into the hold area where Luke is sitting with the princess.

> HAN
> (*to Luke*)
> Come on, buddy, we're not out of this yet!

INT. *MILLENNIUM FALCON* – GUNPORTS – COCKPIT

Solo climbs into his attack position in the topside gunport.

INT. *MILLENNIUM FALCON* – HOLD AREA

Luke gets up and moves out towards the gunports as Leia heads for the cockpit.

INT. *MILLENNIUM FALCON* – GUNPORTS – COCKPIT

Luke climbs down the ladder into the gunport cockpit, settling into one of the two main laser cannons mounted in large rotating turrets on either side of the ship.

INT. *MILLENNIUM FALCON* – SOLO'S GUNPORT

Han adjusts his headset as he sits before the controls of his laser cannon, then speaks into the attached microphone.

> HAN
> (*to Luke*)
> You in, kid? Okay, stay sharp!

INT. *MILLENNIUM FALCON* – GUNPORTS – COCKPIT

Chewbacca and Princess Leia search the heavens for the attacking TIE fighters. The Wookiee pulls back on the speed controls as the ship bounces slightly.

INT. MILLENNIUM FALCON – SOLO'S GUNPORT – COCKPIT

Computer graphic readouts form on Solo's target screen, as Han reaches for controls.

INT. *MILLENNIUM FALCON* – GUNPORT – COCKPIT

Luke sits in readiness for the attack, his hand on the laser cannon's control button.

INT. *MILLENNIUM FALCON* – COCKPIT

Chewbacca spots the enemy ships and barks.

> LEIA
> (*into intercom*)
> Here they come!

INT. COCKPIT – POV SPACE

The Imperial TIE fighters move towards the Millennium Falcon, one each veering off to the left and right of the pirateship.

INT. TIE FIGHTER – COCKPIT

The stars whip past behind the Imperial pilot as he adjusts his maneuvering joystick.

EXT. *MILLENNIUM FALCON* – IN SPACE

The TIE fighter races past the Falcon, *firing laser beams as it passes.*

INT. *MILLENNIUM FALCON* – HOLD AREA

Threepio is seated in the hold area, next to Artoo-Detoo. The pirateship bounces and vibrates as the power goes out in the room and then comes back on.

INT. *MILLENNIUM FALCON* – COCKPIT – GUNPORTS

A TIE fighter maneuvers in front of Han, who follows it and fires at it with the laser cannon. Luke does likewise, as the fighter streaks into view. The ship has suffered a minor hit, and bounces slightly.

EXT. SPACE

Two TIE fighters dive down towards the pirateship.

INT. *MILLENNIUM FALCON* – GUNPORTS

Luke fires at an unseen fighter.

> **LUKE**
> They're coming in too fast!

EXT. SPACE – *MILLENNIUM FALCON*, TIE FIGHTERS

Pan with pirateship as two TIE fighters charge through the background. Laserbolts streak from all the craft.

INT. *MILLENNIUM FALCON* – CHEWBACCA

The ship shudders as a laserbolt hits very close to the cockpit. The Wookiee chatters something to Leia.

EXT. TIE FIGHTER – SPACE

Full shot of a TIE fighter as it moves fast through the frame, firing on the pirate starship.

EXT. SPACE — TIE FIGHTERS

The two TIE fighters fire a barrage of laser beams at the pirateship.

INT. *MILLENNIUM FALCON* — MAIN PASSAGEWAY

A laserbolt streaks into the side of the pirateship. The ship lurches violently, throwing poor Threepio into a cabinet full of small computer chips.

> ### THREEPIO
> Oooh!

INT. *MILLENNIUM FALCON* COCKPIT GUNPORTS

Leia watches the computer readouts as Chewbacca manipulates the ship's controls.

> ### LEIA
> We've lost lateral controls.

> ### HAN
> Don't worry, she'll hold together.

An enemy laserbolt hits the pirateship's control panel, causing it to blow out in a shower of sparks.

> ### HAN
> *(to ship)*
> You hear me, baby? Hold together!

Artoo-Detoo advances towards the smoking, sparking control panel, dousing the inferno by spraying it with fire retardant, beeping all the while.

INT. *MILLENNIUM FALCON* — GUNPORT

Luke swivels in his gun mount, following the TIE fighter with his laser cannon.

INT. *MILLENNIUM FALCON* — GUNPORT

Solo aims his laser cannon at the enemy fighters.

EXT. SPACE

A TIE fighter streaks in front of the starship.

INT. *MILLENNIUM FALCON* – COCKPIT

Leia watches the TIE ship fly over.

EXT. SPACE

A TIE fighter heads right for the pirateship, then zooms overhead.

INT. *MILLENNIUM FALCON* – GUNPORTS

Luke follows the TIE fighter across his field of view, firing laser beams from his cannon.

EXT. TIE FIGHTER

A TIE fighter dives past the pirateship.

INT. *MILLENNIUM FALCON* – GUNPORTS

Luke fires at a TIE fighter. At his port, Han follows a fighter in his sights, releasing a blast of laserfire. He connects, and the fighter explodes into fiery dust. Han laughs victoriously.

EXT. SPACE

Two TIE fighters move towards and over the Millennium Falcon, *unleashing a barrage of laserbolts at the ship.*

INT. *MILLENNIUM FALCON* – GUNPORTS

Another TIE fighter moves in on the pirateship and Luke, smiling, fires the laser cannon at it, scoring a spectacular direct hit.

LUKE

Got him! I got him!

Han turns and gives Luke a victory wave which Luke gleefully returns.

HAN

Great kid! Don't get cocky.

Han turns back to his laser cannon.

EXT. SPACE

Two more TIE fighters cross in front of the pirateship.

INT. *MILLENNIUM FALCON* – COCKPIT

While Chewbacca manipulates the controls, Leia turns, looking over her shoulder out the ports.

LEIA
There are still two more of them out there!

EXT. SPACE

A TIE fighter moves up over the pirateship, firing laserblasts at it.

INT. *MILLENNIUM FALCON* – GUNPORTS

Luke and Han look into their respective projected target screens. An Imperial fighter crosses Solo's port, and Han swivels in his chair, following it with blasts from his laser cannon. Another fighter crosses Luke's port, and he reacts in a like manner, the glow of his target screen lighting his face.

EXT. SPACE

The TIE fighter zooms towards the pirateship, firing destructive blasts at it.

INT. *MILLENNIUM FALCON* – GUNPORTS

Luke fires a laserblast at the approaching enemy fighter, and it bursts into a spectacular explosion. Luke's projected screen gives a readout of the hit. The pirateship bounces slightly as it is struck by enemy fire.

EXT. SPACE – TIE FIGHTER

The last of the attacking Imperial TIE fighters looms in, firing upon the Falcon.

INT. *MILLENNIUM FALCON* – GUNPORT

Solo swivels behind his laser cannon, his aim describing the arc of the

TIE fighter. The fighter comes closer, firing at the pirateship, but a well-aimed blast from Solo's laser cannon hits the attacker, which blows up in a small atomic shower of burning fragments.

> LUKE
> *(laughing)*

That's it! We did it!

The princess jumps up and gives Chewie a congratulatory hug.

> LEIA

We did it!

INT. *MILLENNIUM FALCON* – PASSAGEWAY

Threepio lies on the floor of the ship, completely tangled in the smoking, sparking wires.

> THREEPIO

Help! I think I'm melting!
> *(to Artoo)*

This is all your fault.

Artoo turns his dome from side to side, beeping in response.

EXT. SPACE – *MILLENNIUM FALCON*

The victorious Millennium Falcon *moves off majestically through space.*

INT. DEATH STAR – CONTROL ROOM

Darth Vader strides into the control room, where Tarkin is watching the huge view screen. A sea of stars is before him.

> TARKIN

Are they away?

> VADER

They have just made the jump into hyperspace.

> TARKIN

You're sure the homing beacon is secure aboard their ship? I'm taking an awful risk, Vader. This had better work.

Han, removing his gloves and smiling, is at the controls of the ship. Chewie moves into the aft section to check the damage. Leia is seated near Han.

HAN

Not a bad bit of rescuing, huh? You know, sometimes I even amaze myself.

LEIA

That doesn't sound too hard. Besides, they let us go. It's the only explanation for the ease of our escape.

HAN

Easy . . . you call that easy?

LEIA

They're tracking us!

HAN

Not this ship, sister.

Frustrated, Leia shakes her head.

LEIA

At least the information in Artoo is still intact.

HAN

What's so important? What's he carrying?

LEIA

The technical readouts of that battle station. I only hope that when the data is analyzed, a weakness can be found. It's not over yet!

HAN

It is for me, sister! Look, I ain't in this for your revolution, and I'm not in it for you, Princess. I expect to be well paid. I'm in it for the money!

LEIA

You needn't worry about your reward. If money is all that you love, then that's what you'll receive.

She angrily turns and, as she starts out of the cockpit, passes Luke coming in.

Your friend is quite a mercenary. I wonder if he really cares about anything . . . or anybody.

LUKE

I care!

Luke, shaking his head, sits in the copilot seat. He and Han stare out at the vast blackness of space.

LUKE

So . . . what do you think of her, Han?

HAN

I'm trying not to, kid!

LUKE
(under his breath)

Good . . .

HAN

Still, she's got a lot of spirit. I don't know, what do you think? Do you think a princess and a guy like me . . .

LUKE

No!

He says it with finality and looks away. Han smiles at young Luke's jealousy.

EXT. SPACE AROUND FOURTH MOON OF YAVIN

The battered pirateship drifts into orbit around the planet Yavin and proceeds to one of its tiny green moons.

EXT. FOURTH MOON OF YAVIN

The pirateship soars over the dense jungle.

EXT. MASSASSI OUTPOST

An alert guard, his laser gun in hand, scans the countryside. He sets the gun down and looks towards the temple, barely visible in the foliage.

EXT. MASSASSI OUTPOST — JUNGLE TEMPLE

Rotting in a forest of gargantuan trees, an ancient temple lies shrouded in an eerie mist. The air is heavy with the fantastic cries of unimaginable creatures. Han, Luke, and the others are greeted by the Rebel troops.

Luke and the group ride into the massive temple on an armored military speeder.

INT. MASSASSI — MAIN HANGAR DECK

The military speeder stops in a huge spaceship hangar, set up in the interior of the crumbling temple.

Willard, the commander of the Rebel forces, rushes up to the group and gives Leia a big hug. Everyone is pleased to see her.

> WILLARD
> (holding Leia)
> You're safe! We had feared the worst.

He composes himself, steps back and bows formally.

> WILLARD
> When we heard about Alderaan, we were afraid that you were
> . . . lost along with your father.

> LEIA
> We don't have time for our sorrows, Commander. The battle
> station has surely tracked us here.
> (looking pointedly at Han)
> It's the only explanation for the ease of our escape. You must
> use the information in this R2 unit to plan the attack. It is our
> only hope.

EXT. SPACE

The surface of the Death Star ominously approaches the red planet Yavin.

INT. DEATH STAR — CONTROL ROOM

Grand Moff Tarkin and Lord Darth Vader are interrupted in their discussion by the buzz of the comlink. Tarkin moves to answer the call.

Yes.

VOICE
(*on intercom*)

We are approaching the planet Yavin. The Rebel base is on a moon on the far side. We are preparing to orbit the planet.

EXT. YAVIN – JUNGLE

A lone guard stands in a tower high above the Yavin landscape, surveying the countryside. A mist hangs over the jungle of twisted green.

INT. MASSASSI – WAR-ROOM BRIEFING AREA

Dodonna stands before a large electronic wall display. Leia and several other senators are to one side of the giant readout. The low-ceilinged room is filled with star pilots, navigators, and a sprinkling of R2-type robots. Everyone is listening intently to what Dodonna is saying. Han and Chewbacca are standing near the back.

DODONNA

The battle station is heavily shielded and carries a firepower greater than half the starfleet. Its defenses are designed around a direct large-scale assault. A small one-man fighter should be able to penetrate the outer defense.

Gold Leader, a rough-looking man in his early thirties, stands.

GOLD LEADER
(*to Dodonna*)

Pardon me for asking, sir, but what good are snub fighters going to be against that?

DODONNA

Well, the Empire doesn't consider a small one-man fighter to be any threat, or they'd have a tighter defense. An analysis of the plans provided by Princess Leia has demonstrated a weakness in the battle station.

Artoo-Detoo stands next to a similar robot, makes beeping sounds, and turns his head from right to left.

DODONNA

The approach will not be easy. You are required to maneuver straight down this trench and skim the surface to this point. The target area is only two meters wide. It's a small thermal exhaust port, right below the main port. The shaft leads directly to the reactor system. A precise hit will start a chain reaction which should destroy the station.

A murmur of disbelief runs through the room.

DODONNA

Only a precise hit will set up a chain reaction. The shaft is ray-shielded, so you'll have to use proton torpedoes.

Luke is sitting next to Wedge Antilles, a hotshot pilot about sixteen years old.

WEDGE

That's impossible, even for a computer.

LUKE

It's not impossible. I used to bull's-eye womp rats in my T-sixteen back home. They're not much bigger than two meters.

DODONNA
Man your ships! And may the Force be with you!

The group rises and begins to leave.

INT. SPACE

The Death Star begins to move around the planet towards the tiny green moon.

INT. DEATH STAR

Tarkin and Vader watch the computer-projected screen with interest, as a circle of lights intertwines around one another on the screen showing its position in relation to Yavin and the fourth moon.

DEATH STAR INTERCOM VOICE
Orbiting the planet at maximum velocity. The moon with the Rebel base will be in range in thirty minutes.

VADER
This will be a day long remembered. It has seen the end of Kenobi and will soon see the end of the Rebellion.

INT. MASSASSI OUTPOST — MAIN HANGAR DECK

Luke, Threepio, and little Artoo enter the huge spaceship hangar and hurry along a long line of gleaming spacefighters. Flight crews rush around loading last-minute armaments and unlocking power couplings. In an area isolated from this activity, Luke finds Han and Chewbacca loading small boxes on to an armored speeder.

VOICE
(*over loudspeaker*)
All flight troops, man your stations. All flight troops, man your stations.

Han is deliberately ignoring the activity of the fighter pilots' preparations. Luke is quite saddened at the sight of his friend's departure.

LUKE
So . . . you got your reward and you're just leaving then?

HAN

That's right, yeah! I got some old debts I've got to pay off
with this stuff. Even if I didn't, you don't think I'd be fool
enough to stick around here, do you? Why don't you come
with us? You're pretty good in a fight. I could use you.

LUKE
(*getting angry*)
Come on! Why don't you take a look around? You know
what's about to happen, what they're up against. They could
use a good pilot like you. You're turning your back on them.

HAN

What good's a reward if you ain't around to use it? Besides,
attacking that battle station ain't my idea of courage. It's
more like suicide.

LUKE

All right. Well, take care of yourself, Han . . . guess that's
what you're best at, isn't it?

He goes off and Han hesitates, then calls to him.

HAN

Hey, Luke . . . may the Force be with you!

*Luke turns and sees Han wink at him. Luke lifts his hand in a small
wave and goes off.*

Han turns to Chewie who growls at his captain.

HAN

What're you lookin' at? I know what I'm doing.

INT. MAIN HANGAR DECK – LUKE'S SHIP

Luke, Leia, and Dodonna meet under a huge spacefighter.

LEIA

What's wrong?

LUKE

Oh, it's Han! I don't know, I really thought he'd change his
mind.

LEIA

He's got to follow his own path. No one can choose it for him.

LUKE

I only wish Ben were here.

Leia gives Luke a little kiss, turns, and goes off.

As Luke heads for his ship, another pilot rushes up to him and grabs his arm.

BIGGS

Luke! I don't believe it! How'd you get here . . . are you going out with us?!

LUKE

Biggs! Of course, I'll be up there with you! Listen, have I got some stories to tell you . . .

Red Leader, a rugged, handsome man in his forties, comes up behind Luke and Biggs. He has the confident smile of a born leader.

RED LEADER

Are you . . . Luke Skywalker? Have you been checked out on the Incom T-sixty-five?

BIGGS

Sir, Luke is the best bushpilot in the outer rim territories.

Pilot Leader pats Luke on the back as they stop in front of his fighter.

PILOT LEADER

I met your father once when I was just a boy. He was a great pilot. You'll do all right. If you've got half of your father's skill, you'll do better than all right.

LUKE

Thank you, sir. I'll try.

Red Leader hurries to his own ship.

BIGGS

I've got to get aboard. Listen, you'll tell me your stories when we come back. All right?

LUKE

I told you I'd make it someday, Biggs.

BIGGS
(*going off*)
You did, all right. It's going to be like old times, Luke. We're a couple of shooting stars that'll never be stopped!

Luke laughs and shakes his head in agreement. He heads for his ship.

As Luke begins to climb up the ladder into his sleek, deadly spaceship, the crew Chief, who is working on the craft, points to little Artoo, who is being hoisted into a socket on the back of the fighter.

CHIEF

This R2 unit of yours seems a bit beat-up. Do you want a new one?

LUKE

Not on your life! That little droid and I have been through a lot together.
(*to Artoo*)
You okay, Artoo?

The crewmen lower Artoo-Detoo into the craft. Now a part of the exterior shell of the starship, the little droid beeps that he is fine.

Luke climbs up into the cockpit of his fighter and puts on his helmet. Threepio looks on from the floor of the massive hangar as the crewmen secure his little electronic partner into Luke's X-wing. It's an emotion-filled moment as Artoo beeps goodbye.

CHIEF

Okay, easy she goes!

THREEPIO

Hang on tight, Artoo, you've got to come back.

Artoo beeps in agreement.

THREEPIO

You wouldn't want my life to get boring, would you?

Artoo whistles his reply.

All final preparations are made for the approaching battle. The hangar is buzzing with the last-minute activity as the pilots and crewmen alike make their final adjustments.

The hum of activity is occasionally trespassed by the distorted voice of the loudspeaker issuing commands. Coupling hoses are disconnected from the ships as they are fueled. Cockpit shields roll smoothly into place over each pilot. A signalman, holding red guiding lights, directs the ships. Luke, a trace of a smile gracing his lips, peers about through his goggles.

BEN'S VOICE
Luke, the Force will be with you.

Luke is confused at the voice and taps his headphones.

EXT. MASSASSI OUTPOST – JUNGLE

All that can be seen of the fortress is a lone guard standing on a small pedestal jutting out above the dense jungle. The muted, gruesome crying sounds that naturally permeate this eerie purgatory are overwhelmed by the thundering din of ion rockets as four silver starships catapult from the foliage in a tight formation and disappear into the morning cloud cover.

INT. MASSASSI OUTPOST – WAR ROOM

The princess, Threepio, and a field commander sit quietly before the giant display showing the planet Yavin and its four moons. The red dot that represents the Death Star moves ever closer to the system. A series of green dots appears around the fourth moon. A din of indistinct chatter fills the war room.

MASSASSI INTERCOM VOICE
Stand-by alert. Death Star approaching. Estimated time to firing range, fifteen minutes.

EXT. SPACE

The Death Star slowly moves behind the massive yellow surface of Yavin in the foreground, as many X-wing fighters flying in formation zoom towards us and out of the frame.

EXT. SPACE — ANOTHER ANGLE

Light from a distant sun creates an eerie atmospheric glow around a huge planet, Yavin. Rebel fighters flying in formation settle ominously in the foreground and very slowly pull away.

INT. RED LEADER STARSHIP — COCKPIT

Red Leader lowers his visor and adjusts his gun sights, looking to each side at his wingmen.

RED LEADER

All Wings report in.

INT. ANOTHER COCKPIT

One of the Rebel fighters checks in through his mike.

RED TEN

Red Ten standing by.

INT. BIGGS'S COCKPIT

Biggs checks his fighter's controls, alert and ready for combat.

RED SEVEN
(over Biggs's headset)

Red Seven standing by.

BIGGS

Red Three standing by.

INT. PORKINS'S COCKPIT

PORKINS

Red Six standing by.

RED NINE
(over headset)

Red Nine standing by.

INT. WEDGE'S FIGHTER — COCKPIT

> WEDGE

Red Two standing by.

INT. LUKE'S X-WING FIGHTER — COCKPIT

> RED ELEVEN
> (*over headset*)

Red Eleven standing by.

> LUKE

Red Five standing by.

EXT. LUKE'S X-WING FIGHTER

Artoo-Detoo, in position outside of the fighter, turns his head from side to side and makes beeping sounds.

INT. RED LEADER'S FIGHTER — COCKPIT

> RED LEADER

Lock S-foils in attack position.

EXT. SPACE

The group of X-wing fighters moves in formation towards the Death Star, unfolding the wings and locking them into the X position.

INT. BIGGS'S COCKPIT

> RED LEADER
> (*over headset*)

We're passing through their magnetic field.

INT. RED LEADER'S COCKPIT

> RED LEADER

Hold tight!

INT. LUKE'S X-WING FIGHTER — COCKPIT

Luke adjusts his controls as he concentrates on the approaching Death

Star. The ship begins to be buffeted slightly.

> RED LEADER
> (*over headset*)

Switch your deflectors on.

INT. ANOTHER COCKPIT

> RED LEADER
> (*over headset*)

Double front!

EXT. SPACE

The fighters, now X-shaped darts, move in formation. The Death Star now appears to be a small moon growing rapidly in size as the Rebel fighters approach. Complex patterns on the metallic surface begin to become visible. A large dish antenna is built into the surface on one side.

INT. WEDGE'S COCKPIT

Wedge is amazed and slightly frightened at the awesome spectacle.

> WEDGE

Look at the size of that thing!

> RED LEADER
> (*over headset*)

Cut the chatter, Red Two.

INT. RED LEADER'S COCKPIT

> RED LEADER

Accelerate to attack speed. This is it, boys!

EXT. SPACE

As the fighters move closer to the Death Star, the awesome size of the gargantuan Imperial fortress is revealed. Half of the deadly space station is in shadow and this area sparkles with thousands of small lights running in thin lines and occasionally grouped in large clusters; somewhat like a city at night as seen from a weather satellite.

133

INT. GOLD LEADER'S COCKPIT

> GOLD LEADER
>
> Red Leader, this is Gold Leader.

> RED LEADER
> (over headset)
>
> I copy, Gold Leader.

> GOLD LEADER
>
> We're starting for the target shaft now.

INT. RED LEADER'S COCKPIT

Red Leader looks around at his wingmen; the Death Star looming in from behind. Two Y-wing fighters bob back and forth in the background. He moves his computer targeting device into position.

> RED LEADER
>
> We're in position. I'm going to cut across the axis and try and draw their fire.

EXT. SPACE

Two squads of Rebel fighters peel off. The X-wings dive towards the Death Star's surface. A thousand lights glow across the dark gray expanse of the huge station.

INT. DEATH STAR

Alarm sirens scream as soldiers scramble to large turbo-powered laser gun emplacements. Electronic drivers rotate the huge guns into position as the crew adjusts their targeting devices.

EXT. SPACE AROUND THE DEATH STAR

Laserbolts streak through the star-filled night. The Rebel X-wing fighters move in towards the Imperial base, as the Death Star aims its massive laser guns at the Rebel forces and fires.

INT. MASSASSI OUTPOST — WAR ROOM

Princess Leia listens to the battle over the intercom. Threepio is at her side.

> WEDGE
> *(over war-room speaker system)*
> Heavy fire, boss! Twenty-three degrees.

> RED LEADER
> *(over speaker)*
> I see it. Stay low.

EXT. SPACE

An X-wing zooms across the surface of the Death Star.

INT. DEATH STAR

Technical crews scurry here and there loading last-minute armaments and unlocking power cables.

INT. WEDGE'S COCKPIT

Wedge maneuvers his fighter towards the menacing Death Star.

EXT. SPACE

X-wings continue in their attack course on the Death Star.

INT. LUKE'S X-WING FIGHTER — COCKPIT

Luke nosedives radically, starting his attack on the monstrous fortress. The Death Star surface streaks past the cockpit window.

> LUKE
> This is Red Five! I'm going in!

EXT. SPACE

Luke's X-wing races towards the Death Star. Laserbolts streak from Luke's weapons, creating a huge fireball explosion on the dim surface.

INT. LUKE'S X-WING FIGHTER — COCKPIT

Terror crosses Luke's face as he realizes he won't be able to pull out in time to avoid the fireball.

BIGGS
(*over headset*)
Luke, pull out!

EXT. SURFACE OF THE DEATH STAR

Luke's ship emerges from the fireball, with the leading edges of his wings slightly scorched.

INT. BIGGS'S COCKPIT

BIGGS
Are you all right?

INT. LUKE'S X-WING FIGHTER – COCKPIT

Luke adjusts his controls and breathes a sigh of relief. Flak bursts outside the cockpit window.

LUKE
I got a little cooked, but I'm okay.

EXT. SURFACE OF THE DEATH STAR

Rebel fighters continue to strafe the Death Star's surface with laserbolts.

INT. DEATH STAR

Walls buckle and cave in. Troops and equipment are blown in all directions. Stormtroopers stagger out of the rubble. Standing in the middle of the chaos, a vision of calm and foreboding, is Darth Vader. One of his Astro-Officers rushes up to him.

ASTRO-OFFICER
We count thirty Rebel ships, Lord Vader. But they're so small they're evading our turbo-lasers!

VADER

We'll have to destroy them ship to ship. Get the crews to their fighters.

INT. DEATH STAR

Smoke belches from the giant laser guns as they wind up their turbine generators to create sufficient power. The crew rushes about preparing for another blast. Even the troopers' head gear is not adequate to protect them from the overwhelming noise of the monstrous weapon. One trooper bangs his helmet with his hand in an attempt to stop the ringing.

INT. RED LEADER'S X-WING – COCKPIT – TRAVELING

Red Leader flies through a heavy hail of flak.

RED LEADER

Luke, let me know when you're going in.

INT. LUKE'S X-WING – COCKPIT – TRAVELING

The Red Leader's X-wing flies past Luke as he puts his nose down and starts his attack dive.

LUKE

I'm on my way in now . . .

RED LEADER

Watch yourself! There's a lot of fire coming from the right side of that deflection tower.

LUKE

I'm on it.

EXT. SURFACE OF THE DEATH STAR

Luke flings his X-wing into a twisting dive across the horizon and down on to the dim gray surface.

EXT. LUKE'S X-WING – TRAVELING

A shot hurls from Luke's guns. Laserbolts streak towards the onrushing Death Star's surface. Several small radar emplacements erupt in flame.

Laserfire erupts from a protruding tower on the surface.

INT. LUKE'S X-WING — COCKPIT — TRAVELING

The blurry Death Star's surface races past the cockpit windows as a big smile sweeps across Luke's face at the success of his run. Flak thunders on all sides of him.

EXT. SURFACE OF THE DEATH STAR

The Death Star's superstructure races past Luke as he maneuvers his craft through a wall of laserfire and peels away from the surface towards the heavens.

INT. DEATH STAR

The thunder and smoke of the big guns reverberate throughout the massive structure. Many soldiers rush about in the smoke and chaos, silhouetted by the almost continual flash of explosions.

INT. BIGGS'S COCKPIT — TRAVELING

Biggs dives through a forest of radar domes, antennae, and gun towers as he shoots low across the Death Star's surface. A dense barrage of laserfire streaks by on all sides.

INT. DEATH STAR

Imperial star pilots dash in unison to a line of small auxiliary hatches that lead to Imperial TIE fighters.

INT. MASSASSI OUTPOST — WAR ROOM

Princess Leia, surrounded by her generals and aides, paces nervously before a lighted computer table. On all sides technicians work in front of many lighted glass walls. Dodonna watches quietly from one corner. One of the officers working over a screen speaks into his headset.

> CONTROL OFFICER
> Squad leaders, we've picked up a new group of signals.
> Enemy fighters coming your way.

INT. LUKE'S X-WING FIGHTER – COCKPIT – TRAVELING

Luke looks around to see if he can spot the approaching Imperial fighter.

> **LUKE**
> My scope's negative. I don't see anything.

INT. RED LEADER'S X-WING – COCKPIT – TRAVELING

The Death Star's surface sweeps past as Red Leader searches the sky for the Imperial fighter. Flak pounds at his ship.

> **RED LEADER**
> Keep up your visual scanning. With all this jamming, they'll be on top of you before your scope can pick them up.

EXT. SURFACE OF THE DEATH STAR

Silhouetted against the rim lights of the Death Star horizon, four ferocious Imperial TIE ships dive on the Rebel fighters. Two of the TIE fighters peel off and drop out of frame. Pan with the remaining two TIE ships.

INT. BIGGS'S COCKPIT – TRAVELING

Biggs panics when he discovers a TIE ship on his tail. The horizon in the background twists around as he peels off, hoping to lose the Imperial fighter.

INT. RED LEADER'S COCKPIT

> **RED LEADER**
> Biggs! You've picked one up . . . watch it!

> **BIGGS**
> I can't see it! Where is he?!

EXT. SPACE AROUND THE DEATH STAR

Biggs zooms off the surface and into space, closely followed by an Imperial TIE fighter. The TIE ship fires several laserbolts at Biggs, but misses.

INT. BIGGS'S COCKPIT – TRAVELING

Biggs sees the TIE ship behind him and swings around, trying to avoid him.

> BIGGS
> He's on me tight, I can't shake him . . . I can't shake him.

EXT. SPACE AROUND THE DEATH STAR

Biggs, flying at high altitude, peels off and dives towards the Death Star's surface, but he is unable to lose the TIE fighter, who sticks close to his tail.

INT. X-WING FIGHTER – COCKPIT – TRAVELING

Luke is flying upside down. He rotates his ship around to a normal attitude as he comes out of his dive.

> LUKE
> Hang on, Biggs, I'm coming in.

EXT. SPACE AROUND THE DEATH STAR

Biggs and the tailing TIE ship dive for the surface, now followed by a fast-gaining Luke. After Biggs dives out of sight, Luke chases the Imperial fighter.

EXT. SURFACE OF THE DEATH STAR

In the foreground, the Imperial fighter races across the Death Star's surface, closely followed by Luke in the background.

INT. LUKE'S X-WING FIGHTER – COCKPIT – TRAVELING

There is a shot from Luke's X-wing of the TIE ship exploding in a mass of flames.

> LUKE
> Got him!

INT. DEATH STAR

Darth Vader strides purposefully down a Death Star corridor, flanked by Imperial stormtroopers.

> VADER

Several fighters have broken off from the main group. Come
with me!

INT. MASSASSI OUTPOST – WAR ROOM

*A concerned Princess Leia, Threepio, Dodonna, and other officers of the
Rebellion stand around the huge round readout screen, listening to the
ship-to-ship communication on the room's loudspeaker.*

> BIGGS
> (*over speaker*)

Pull in! Luke . . . pull in!

> WEDGE
> (*over speaker*)

Watch your back, Luke!

INT. LUKE'S X-WING FIGHTER – COCKPIT

> WEDGE
> (*over headset*)

Watch your back! Fighters above you, coming in!

EXT. SPACE

*Luke's ship soars away from the Death Star's surface as he spots the
tailing TIE fighter.*

INT. TIE FIGHTER'S COCKPIT

The TIE pilot takes aim at Luke's X-wing.

EXT. SPACE

*The Imperial TIE fighter pilot scores a hit on Luke's ship. Fire breaks
out on the right side of the X-wing.*

INT. LUKE'S X-WING FIGHTER – COCKPIT

Luke looks out of his cockpit at the flames on his ship.

LUKE

I'm hit, but not bad.

EXT. LUKE'S X-WING FIGHTER

Smoke pours out from behind Artoo-Detoo.

LUKE'S VOICE

Artoo, see what you can do with it. Hang on back there.

Green laserfire moves past the beeping little robot as his head turns.

INT. LUKE'S X-WING – COCKPIT

Luke nervously works his controls.

RED LEADER
(*over headset*)

Red Six . . .

INT. MASSASSI OUTPOST – WAR ROOM

In the war room, Leia stands frozen as she listens and worries about Luke.

RED LEADER
(*over speaker*)

Can you see Red Five?

RED TEN
(*over speaker*)

There's a heavy fire zone on this side. Red Five, where are you?

INT. LUKE'S X-WING – COCKPIT

Luke spots the TIE fighters behind him and soars away from the Death Star's surface.

LUKE

I can't shake him!

EXT. SURFACE OF THE DEATH STAR

*Luke's ship soars closer to the surface of the Death Star, an Imperial
TIE fighter closing in on him in hot pursuit.*

INT. WEDGE'S COCKPIT

The Death Star whips below Wedge.

> WEDGE

I'm on him, Luke!

INT. LUKE'S X-WING – COCKPIT

> WEDGE
> (*over headset*)

Hold on!

EXT. SURFACE OF THE DEATH STAR

Wedge dives across the horizon towards Luke and the TIE fighter.

INT. WEDGE'S COCKPIT

Wedge moves his X-wing in rapidly.

INT. LUKE'S X-WING – COCKPIT

Luke reacts frantically.

> LUKE

Blast it! Wedge, where are you?

INT. TIE FIGHTER – COCKPIT

*The fighter pilot watches Wedge's X-wing approach. Another X-wing
joins him, and both unleash a volley of laserfire on the Imperial fighter.*

EXT. SPACE

*The TIE fighter explodes, filling the screen with white light. Luke's ship
can be seen far in the distance.*

INT. LUKE'S X-WING — COCKPIT

Luke looks about in relief.

> LUKE
>
> Thanks, Wedge.

INT. MASSASSI OUTPOST — WAR ROOM

Leia, Threepio, Dodonna, and other Rebel officers are listening to the Rebel fighters' radio transmissions over the war-room intercom.

> BIGGS
> (*over speaker*)
>
> Good shooting, Wedge!

> GOLD LEADER
> (*over speaker*)
>
> Red Leader . . .

INT. GOLD LEADER'S Y-WING — COCKPIT

Gold Leader peels off and starts towards the long trenches at the Death Star's surface pole.

> GOLD LEADER
>
> . . . This is Gold Leader. We're starting our attack run.

EXT. SPACE AROUND THE DEATH STAR

Three Y-wing fighters of the Gold group dive out of the stars towards the Death Star's surface.

INT. MASSASSI OUTPOST — WAR ROOM

Leia and the others are grouped around the screen, as technicians move about attending to their duties.

> RED LEADER
> (*over speaker*)
>
> I copy, Gold Leader. Move into position.

EXT. SPACE AROUND THE DEATH STAR

Three Imperial TIE ships in precise formation dive towards the Death Star's surface.

INT. DARTH VADER'S COCKPIT

Darth Vader calmly adjusts his control stick as the stars whip past in the window above his head.

> VADER
>
> Stay in attack formation!

INT. MASSASSI OUTPOST – WAR ROOM

Technicians are seated at the computer readout table.

> GOLD LEADER
> (*over speaker*)
>
> The exhaust port is –

INT. GOLD LEADER'S Y-WING – COCKPIT

> GOLD LEADER
>
> – marked and locked in!

EXT. SPACE AROUND THE DEATH STAR

Gold Leader approaches the surface and pulls out to skim the surface of the huge station. The ship moves into a deep trench, firing laserbolts. The surface streaks past as laserfire is returned by the Death Star.

INT. GOLD FIVE'S Y-WING – COCKPIT – TRAVELING

Gold Five is a pilot in his early fifties with a very battered helmet that looks like it's been through many battles. He looks around to see if enemy ships are near. His fighter is buffeted by Imperial flak.

INT. GOLD LEADER'S Y-WING – COCKPIT

Gold Leader races down the enormous trench that leads to the exhaust port. Laserbolts blast towards him in increasing numbers, occasionally exploding near the ship, causing it to bounce about.

GOLD LEADER
Switch power to front deflection screens.

EXT. SURFACE OF THE DEATH STAR

Three Y-wings skim the Death Star's surface deep in the trench, as laserbolts streak past on all sides.

EXT. DEATH STAR SURFACE – GUN EMPLACEMENT

An exterior surface gun blazes away at the oncoming Rebel fighters.

INT. GOLD LEADER'S Y-WING – COCKPIT

GOLD LEADER
How many guns do you think, Gold Five?

INT. MASSASSI OUTPOST – WAR ROOM

GOLD FIVE
(*over speaker*)
I'd say about twenty guns. Some on the surface, some on the towers.

Leia, Threepio, and the technicians view the projected-target screen, as red and blue target lights glow. The red target near the center blinks on and off.

MASSASSI INTERCOM VOICE
(*over speaker*)
Death Star will be in range in five minutes.

EXT. SURFACE OF THE DEATH STAR

The three Y-wing fighters race towards camera and zoom overhead through a hail of laserfire.

INT. GOLD LEADER'S Y-WING – COCKPIT

Gold Leader pulls his computer targeting device down in front of his eye. Laserbolts continue to batter the Rebel craft.

> GOLD LEADER

Switch to targeting computer.

INT. GOLD TWO'S Y-WING – COCKPIT

Gold Two, a younger pilot, about Luke's age, pulls down his targeting eye viewer and adjusts it. His ship shudders under intense laser barrage.

> GOLD TWO

Computer's locked. Getting a signal.

As the fighters begin to approach the target area, suddenly all the laserfire stops. An eerie calm clings over the trench as the surface whips past in a blur.

> GOLD TWO

The guns . . . they've stopped!

EXT. SURFACE OF THE DEATH STAR

Two Y-wings zoom down the Death Star's trench.

INT. GOLD FIVE'S COCKPIT

Gold Five looks behind him.

> GOLD FIVE

Stabilize your rear deflectors. Watch for enemy fighters.

INT. GOLD LEADER'S Y-WING – COCKPIT

> GOLD LEADER

They're coming in! Three marks at two-ten.

EXT. SPACE AROUND THE DEATH STAR

Three Imperial TIE ships, Darth Vader in the center flanked by two wingmen, dive in precise formation almost vertically toward the Death Star's surface.

INT. DARTH VADER'S COCKPIT

Darth Vader calmly adjusts his control stick as the stars zoom by.

VADER
I'll take them myself! Cover me!

WINGMAN'S VOICE
(over speaker)
Yes, sir.

EXT. SPACE AROUND THE DEATH STAR SURFACE

Three TIE fighters zoom across the surface of the Death Star.

INT. DARTH VADER'S COCKPIT

*Vader lines up Gold Two in his targeting computer. Vader's hands grip
the control stick as he presses the button.*

INT. GOLD TWO'S Y-WING – COCKPIT

The cockpit explodes around Gold Two. His head falls forward.

EXT. SPACE AROUND THE DEATH STAR

As Gold Two's ship explodes, debris is flung out into space.

INT. GOLD LEADER'S Y-WING – COCKPIT

Gold Leader looks over his shoulder at the scene.

INT. DEATH STAR TRENCH

The three TIE fighters race along in the trench in a tight formation.

INT. GOLD LEADER'S Y-WING – COCKPIT

Gold Leader panics.

GOLD LEADER
(into mike)
I can't maneuver!

INT. GOLD FIVE'S Y-WING – COCKPIT

Gold Five, the old veteran, tries to calm Gold Leader.

GOLD FIVE

Stay on target.

INT. GOLD LEADER'S Y-WING – COCKPIT

The Death Star races by outside the cockpit window as he adjusts his targeting device.

GOLD LEADER

We're too close.

INT. GOLD FIVE'S Y-WING – COCKPIT

The older pilot remains calm.

GOLD FIVE

Stay on target!

INT. GOLD LEADER'S Y-WING – COCKPIT

Now he's really panicked.

GOLD LEADER

Loosen up!

INT. DARTH VADER'S COCKPIT

Vader calmly adjusts his targeting computer and pushes the fire button.

INT. GOLD LEADER'S Y-WING – COCKPIT

Gold Leader's ship is hit by Vader's lasers.

EXT. SURFACE OF THE DEATH STAR

Gold Leader explodes in a ball of flames, throwing debris in all directions.

INT. GOLD FIVE'S Y-WING – COCKPIT

Gold Five moves in on the exhaust port.

GOLD FIVE

Gold Five to Red Leader . . .

INT. LUKE'S X-WING FIGHTER — COCKPIT

Luke looks over his shoulder at the action outside of his cockpit.

> GOLD FIVE
> (*over headset*)
> Lost Tiree, lost Dutch.

INT. RED LEADER'S COCKPIT

> RED LEADER
> I copy, Gold Five.

INT. GOLD FIVE'S Y-WING — COCKPIT

> GOLD FIVE
> They came from behind . . .

EXT. SURFACE OF THE DEATH STAR

One of the engines explodes on Gold Five's Y-wing fighter, blazing out of control. He dives past the horizon towards the Death Star's surface, passing a TIE fighter during his descent. Gold Five, a veteran of countless campaigns, spins towards his death.

INT. LUKE'S X-WING FIGHTER — COCKPIT

Luke looks nervously about him at the explosive battle.

INT. DEATH STAR — CONTROL ROOM

Grand Moff Tarkin and a Chief Officer stand in the Death Star's control room.

> OFFICER
> We've analyzed their attack, sir, and there is a danger. Should I have your ship standing by?

> TARKIN
> Evacuate? In our moment of triumph? I think you overestimate their chances!

Tarkin turns to the computer readout screen. Flames move around the green disk at the center of the screen; numbers read across the bottom.

VOICE
(*over speaker*)

Rebel base, three minutes and closing.

INT. RED LEADER'S COCKPIT

Red Leader looks over at his wingmen.

RED LEADER

Red Group, this is Red Leader.

INT. MASSASSI OUTPOST — WAR ROOM

Dodonna moves to the intercom as he fiddles with the computer keys.

RED LEADER
(*over speaker*)

Rendezvous at mark six point one.

WEDGE
(*over speaker*)

This is Red Two. Flying towards you.

BIGGS
(*over speaker*)

Red Three, standing by.

INT. RED LEADER'S COCKPIT

DODONNA
(*over headset*)

Red Leader, this is Base One. Keep half your group out of range for the next run.

INT. LUKE'S X-WING FIGHTER — COCKPIT

RED LEADER'S VOICE
(*over headset*)

Copy, Base One. Luke, take Red Two and Three. Hold up here and wait for my signal . . . to start your run.

Luke nods his head.

EXT. SPACE AROUND THE DEATH STAR

The X-wing fighters of Luke, Biggs, and Wedge fly in formation high above the Death Star's surface.

INT. LUKE'S X-WING FIGHTER – COCKPIT

Luke peers out from his cockpit.

EXT. SURFACE OF THE DEATH STAR

Two X-wings move across the surface of the Death Star. Red Leader's X-wing drops down to the surface leading to the exhaust port.

INT. RED LEADER'S COCKPIT

Red Leader looks around to watch for the TIE fighters. He begins to perspire.

> RED LEADER
>
> This is it!

EXT. SPACE

Red Leader roams down the trench of the Death Star as lasers streak across the black heavens.

EXT. DEATH STAR SURFACE – GUN EMPLACEMENT

A huge remote-control laser cannon fires at the approaching Rebel fighters.

EXT. DEATH STAR TRENCH

The Rebel fighters evade the Imperial laserblasts.

INT. RED TEN'S COCKPIT

Red Ten looks around for the Imperial fighters.

> RED TEN
>
> We should be able to see it by now.

EXT. DEATH STAR TRENCH

From the cockpits of the Rebel pilots, the surface of the Death Star streaks by, with Imperial laserfire shooting towards them.

INT. RED LEADER'S COCKPIT

> RED LEADER
>
> Keep your eyes open for those fighters!

INT. RED TEN'S COCKPIT

> RED TEN
>
> There's too much interference!

EXT. DEATH STAR TRENCH

Three X-wing fighters move in formation down the Death Star trench.

> RED TEN'S VOICE
>
> Red Five, can you see them from where you are?

INT. LUKE'S X-WING FIGHTER – COCKPIT

Luke looks down at the Death Star's surface below.

> LUKE
>
> No sign of any . . . wait!

INT. RED TEN'S COCKPIT

Red Ten looks up and sees the Imperial fighters.

> LUKE
> (over headset)
>
> Coming in point three-five.

> RED TEN
>
> I see them.

EXT. SURFACE OF THE DEATH STAR

Three TIE fighters, Vader flanked by two wingmen, dive in a tight formation. The sun reflects off their dominant solar fins as they loop towards the Death Star's surface.

INT. RED LEADER'S COCKPIT

Red Leader pulls his targeting device in front of his eyes and makes several adjustments.

> RED LEADER
> I'm in range.

EXT. SURFACE OF THE DEATH STAR

Red Leader's X-wing moves up the Death Star trench.

INT. RED LEADER'S COCKPIT

> RED LEADER
> Target's coming up!

Red Leader looks at his computer target readout screen. He then looks into his targeting device.

> RED LEADER
> Just hold them off for a few seconds.

INT. DARTH VADER'S COCKPIT

Vader adjusts his control lever and dives on the X-wing fighters.

> VADER
> Close up formation.

EXT. DEATH STAR TRENCH

The three TIE fighters move in formation across the Death Star's surface.

INT. RED LEADER'S COCKPIT

> RED LEADER
> Almost there!

Red Leader lines up his target on the targeting device cross-hairs.

EXT. SURFACE OF THE DEATH STAR

Vader and his wingmen zoom down the trench.

INT. DARTH VADER'S COCKPIT

Vader rapidly approaches the two X-wings of Red Ten and Red Twelve. Vader's laser cannon flashes below the view of the front porthole. The X-wings show in the center of Vader's computer screen.

EXT. SPACE

Red Twelve's X-wing fighter is hit by Vader's laserfire, and it explodes into flames against the trench.

INT. RED TEN'S COCKPIT

Red Ten works at his controls furiously, trying to avoid Vader's fighter behind him.

>   RED TEN
>   You'd better let her loose.

INT. RED LEADER'S COCKPIT

Red Leader is concentrating on his targeting device.

>   RED LEADER
>   Almost there!

INT. RED TEN'S COCKPIT

Red Ten panics.

>   RED TEN
>   I can't hold them!

EXT. SURFACE OF THE DEATH STAR

Vader and his wingmen whip through the trench in pursuit of the Rebel fighters.

INT. DARTH VADER'S COCKPIT

Vader coolly pushes the fire button on his control stick.

INT. RED TEN'S COCKPIT

Darth Vader's well-aimed laserfire proves to be unavoidable, and strikes Red Ten's ship. Red Ten screams in anguish and pain.

EXT. SPACE AROUND THE DEATH STAR

Red Ten's ship explodes and bursts into flames.

INT. RED LEADER'S COCKPIT

Grimly, Red Leader takes careful aim and watches his computer targeting device, which shows the target lined up in the cross-hairs, and fires.

INT. RED LEADER'S COCKPIT

RED LEADER

It's away!

EXT. DEATH STAR SURFACE

Red Leader's X-wing pulls up just before a huge explosion billows out of the trench.

INT. DEATH STAR

An armed Imperial stormtrooper is knocked to the floor from the attack explosion. Other troopers scurrying about the corridors are knocked against the wall and lose their balance.

INT. MASSASSI OUTPOST — WAR ROOM

Leia and the others stare at the computer screen.

RED NINE'S VOICE
(*over speaker*)

It's a hit!

RED LEADER
(*over speaker*)

Negative.

INT. RED LEADER'S COCKPIT

Red Leader looks back at the receding Death Star. Tiny explosions are visible in the distance.

RED LEADER
Negative! It didn't go in, it just impacted on the surface.

EXT. SPACE AROUND THE DEATH STAR – TIE FIGHTER

Darth Vader peels off in pursuit as Red Leader's X-wing passes the Death Star horizon.

INT. DARTH VADER'S COCKPIT

Vader swings his ship around for his next kill.

INT. RED LEADER'S COCKPIT

LUKE
(*over headset*)
Red Leader, we're right above you. Turn to point –

INT. LUKE'S X-WING FIGHTER – COCKPIT

Luke tries to spot Red Leader. He looks down at the Death Star's surface.

LUKE
– oh-five; we'll cover for you.

RED LEADER
(*over headset*)

Stay there . . .

INT. RED LEADER'S COCKPIT

A wary Red Leader looks about nervously.

RED LEADER

. . . I just lost my starboard engine.

INT. LUKE'S X-WING FIGHTER — COCKPIT

Luke looks excitedly towards Red Leader's X-wing.

RED LEADER
(*over headset*)

Get set up for your attack run.

INT. DARTH VADER'S COCKPIT

Vader's gloved hands make contact with the control sticks, and he presses their firing buttons.

INT. RED LEADER'S COCKPIT

Red Leader fights to gain control of his ship.

EXT. SPACE AROUND THE DEATH STAR

Laserbolts are firing from Vader's TIE fighter, connecting with Red Leader's Rebel X-wing fighter. Red Leader buys it, creating a tremendous explosion far below. He screams and is destroyed.

INT. LUKE'S X-WING FIGHTER — COCKPIT

Luke looks out the window of his X-wing at the explosion far below. For the first time, he feels the helplessness of his situation.

INT. DEATH STAR

Grand Moff Tarkin casts a sinister eye at the computer screen.

DEATH STAR INTERCOM VOICE

Rebel base, one minute and closing.

INT. MASSASSI OUTPOST — WAR ROOM

Dodonna and Princess Leia, with Threepio beside them, listen intently to the talk between the pilots. The room is grim after Red Leader's death. Princess Leia nervously paces the room.

LUKE
(*over speaker*)
Biggs, Wedge, let's close it up. We're going in. We're going in full throttle.

INT. WEDGE'S COCKPIT

The horizon twists as Wedge begins to pull out.

WEDGE
Right with you, boss.

EXT. SPACE AROUND THE DEATH STAR

The two X-wings peel off against a background of stars and dive towards the Death Star.

INT. BIGGS'S COCKPIT

BIGGS
Luke, at that speed will you be able to pull out in time?

INT. LUKE'S X-WING FIGHTER – COCKPIT

LUKE
It'll be just like Beggar's Canyon back home.

EXT. SPACE AROUND THE DEATH STAR

The three X-wings move in, unleashing a barrage of laserfire. Laserbolts are returned from the Death Star.

INT. BIGGS'S COCKPIT

Luke's lifelong friend struggles with his controls.

BIGGS
We'll stay back far enough to cover you.

INT. LUKE'S COCKPIT

Flak and laserbolts flash outside Luke's cockpit window.

                    WEDGE
                  (*over headset*)
My scope shows the tower, but I can't see the exhaust port!
Are you sure the computer can hit it?

EXT. DEATH STAR – GUN EMPLACEMENT

The Death Star's laser cannon slowly rotates as it shoots laserbolts.

INT. LUKE'S X-WING FIGHTER – COCKPIT

*Luke looks around for the Imperial TIE fighters. He thinks for a
moment and then moves his targeting device into position.*

                      LUKE
Watch yourself! Increase speed full throttle!

INT. WEDGE'S COCKPIT

Wedge looks excitedly about for any sign of the TIE fighters.

                    WEDGE
What about that tower?

INT. LUKE'S X-WING FIGHTER – COCKPIT

                      LUKE
You worry about those fighters! I'll worry about the tower!

EXT. DEATH STAR SURFACE

Luke's X-wing streaks through the trench, firing lasers.

INT. LUKE'S X-WING FIGHTER – COCKPIT

*Luke breaks into a nervous sweat as the laserfire is returned, nicking one
of his wings close to the engine.*

                      LUKE
                    (*to Artoo*)
Artoo . . . that, that stabilizer's broken loose again. See if you
can't lock it down!

EXT. LUKE'S X-WING FIGHTER

Artoo works to repair the damage. The canyon wall rushes by in the background, making his delicate task seem even more precarious.

EXT. DEATH STAR

Two laser cannons are firing on the Rebel fighters.

INT. WEDGE'S COCKPIT

Wedge looks up and sees the TIE ships.

INT. LUKE'S X-WING FIGHTER – COCKPIT

Luke's targeting device marks off the distance to the target.

EXT. SPACE AROUND THE DEATH STAR

Vader and his wingmen zoom closer.

INT. DARTH VADER'S COCKPIT

Vader adjusts his controls and fires laserbolts at two X-wings flying down the trench. He scores a direct hit on Wedge.

INT. MASSASSI OUTPOST – WAR ROOM

Leia and the others are grouped around the computer board.

> **WEDGE**
> (*over speaker*)
> I'm hit! I can't stay with you.

> **LUKE**
> (*over speaker*)
> Get clear, Wedge.

INT. LUKE'S X-WING FIGHTER – COCKPIT

> **LUKE**
> You can't do any more good back there!

INT. WEDGE'S COCKPIT

                         WEDGE
    Sorry!

EXT. SPACE AROUND THE DEATH STAR

Wedge pulls his crippled X-wing back away from the battle.

INT. DARTH VADER'S COCKPIT

Vader watches the escape but issues a command to his wingmen.

                         VADER
    Let him go! Stay on the leader!

EXT. SPACE AROUND THE DEATH STAR

Luke's X-wing speeds down the trench; the three TIE fighters, still in perfect unbroken formation, tail close behind.

INT. BIGGS'S COCKPIT

Biggs looks around at the TIE fighters. He is worried.

                         BIGGS
    Hurry, Luke, they're coming in much faster this time. I can't hold them!

EXT. SPACE AROUND THE DEATH STAR

The three TIE fighters move ever closer, closing in on Luke and Biggs.

INT. LUKE'S X-WING FIGHTER – COCKPIT

Luke looks back anxiously at little Artoo.

                         LUKE
    Artoo, try and increase the power!

EXT. LUKE'S X-WING FIGHTER

Ignoring the bumpy ride, flak, and lasers, a beeping Artoo-Detoo struggles to increase the power, his dome turning from side to side.

EXT. SPACE AROUND THE DEATH STAR

Stealthily, the TIE formation creeps closer.

INT. DARTH VADER'S COCKPIT

Vader adjusts his control stick.

INT. BIGGS'S COCKPIT

Biggs looks around at the TIE fighters.

INT. LUKE'S X-WING FIGHTER – COCKPIT

Luke looks into his targeting device. He moves it away for a moment and ponders its use. He looks back into the computer targeter.

> BIGGS
> (*over headset*)
>
> Hurry up, Luke!

EXT. SPACE AROUND THE DEATH STAR

Vader and his wingmen race through the Death Star's trench. Biggs moves in to cover for Luke, but Vader gains on him.

INT. BIGGS'S COCKPIT

Biggs sees the TIE fighters aiming at him.

> BIGGS
>
> Wait!

INT. DARTH VADER'S COCKPIT

Vader squeezes the fire button on his controls.

INT. BIGGS'S COCKPIT

Biggs's cockpit explodes around him, lighting him in red.

EXT. SURFACE OF THE DEATH STAR

Biggs's ship bursts into a million flaming bits and scatters across the surface.

INT. MASSASSI OUTPOST — WAR ROOM

Leia and the others stare at the computer board.

INT. LUKE'S X-WING — COCKPIT

Luke is stunned by Biggs's death. His eyes are watering, but his anger is also growing.

INT. DEATH STAR — CONTROL ROOM

Grand Moff Tarkin watches the projected-target screen with satisfaction.

> DEATH STAR INTERCOM VOICE
> Rebel base, thirty seconds and closing.

INT. DARTH VADER'S COCKPIT

Vader takes aim on Luke and talks to his wingmen.

> VADER
> I'm on the leader.

EXT. SURFACE OF THE DEATH STAR — LUKE'S SHIP

Luke's ship streaks through the trench of the Death Star.

INT. MASSASSI OUTPOST — WAR ROOM

Princess Leia returns her general's worried and doubtful glances with a solid, grim determination. Threepio seems nervous.

> THREEPIO
> Hang on, Artoo!

INT. LUKE'S X-WING — COCKPIT

Luke concentrates on his targeting device.

EXT. SURFACE OF THE DEATH STAR

Three TIE fighters charge away down the trench towards Luke.

INT. DARTH VADER'S COCKPIT

Vader's fingers curl around the control stick.

INT. LUKE'S X-WING — COCKPIT

Luke adjusts the lens of his targeting device.

EXT. SURFACE OF THE DEATH STAR

Luke's ship charges down the trench.

INT. LUKE'S X-WING — COCKPIT

Luke lines up the yellow cross-hair lines of the targeting device's screen. He looks into the targeting device, then starts at a voice he hears.

> BEN'S VOICE
> Use the Force, Luke.

EXT. SURFACE OF THE DEATH STAR

The Death Star's trench zooms by.

INT. LUKE'S X-WING — COCKPIT

Luke looks up, then starts to look back into the targeting device. He has second thoughts.

> BEN'S VOICE
> Let go, Luke.

A grim determination sweeps across Luke's face as he closes his eyes and starts to mumble Ben's training to himself.

EXT. SURFACE OF THE DEATH STAR

Luke's fighter streaks through the trench.

INT. DARTH VADER'S COCKPIT

> VADER
> The Force is strong with this one!

EXT. SURFACE OF THE DEATH STAR

Vader follows Luke's X-wing down the trench.

INT. LUKE'S X-WING – COCKPIT

Luke looks to the targeting device, then away as he hears Ben's voice.

> BEN'S VOICE
>
> Luke, trust me.

Luke's hand reaches for the control panel and presses the button. The targeting device moves away.

INT. MASSASSI OUTPOST – WAR ROOM

Leia and the others stand watching the projected screen.

> BASE VOICE
> (*over speaker*)
>
> His computer's off. Luke, you switched off your targeting computer. What's wrong?

> LUKE'S VOICE
> (*over speaker*)
>
> Nothing. I'm all right.

EXT. SURFACE OF THE DEATH STAR

Luke's ship streaks ever closer to the exhaust port.

INT. LUKE'S X-WING – COCKPIT

Luke looks at the Death Star's surface streaking by.

EXT. LUKE'S X-WING FIGHTER

Artoo-Detoo turns his head from side to side, beeping in anticipation.

EXT. SURFACE OF THE DEATH STAR

The three TIE fighters, manned by Vader and his two wingmen, follow Luke's X-wing down the trench.

INT. DARTH VADER'S COCKPIT

Vader maneuvers his controls as he looks at his doomed target. He presses the fire buttons on his control sticks. Laserfire shoots towards Luke's X-wing fighter.

EXT. LUKE'S X-WING FIGHTER

A large burst of Vader's laserfire engulfs Artoo. The arms go limp on the smoking little droid as he makes a high-pitched sound.

INT. LUKE'S X-WING FIGHTER – COCKPIT

Luke looks frantically back over his shoulder at Artoo.

EXT. LUKE'S X-WING FIGHTER

Smoke billows out around little Artoo and sparks begin to fly.

> **LUKE**
>
> I've lost Artoo!

Artoo's beeping sounds die out.

INT. MASSASSI OUTPOST – WAR ROOM

Leia and the others stare intently at the projected screen, while Threepio watches the Princess. Lights representing the Death Star and targets glow brightly.

> **MASSASSI INTERCOM VOICE**
>
> The Death Star has cleared the planet. The Death Star has cleared the planet.

INT. DEATH STAR – CONTROL ROOM

Tarkin glares at the projected-target screen.

> **DEATH STAR INTERCOM VOICE**
>
> Rebel base, in range.

> **TARKIN**
>
> You may fire when ready.

Commence primary ignition.

An officer reaches up and pushes buttons on the control panel, as green lighted buttons turn to red.

EXT. SURFACE OF THE DEATH STAR

The three TIE fighters zoom down the Death Star's trench in pursuit of Luke, never breaking formation.

INT. LUKE'S COCKPIT

Luke looks anxiously at the exhaust port.

INT. DARTH VADER'S COCKPIT

Vader adjusts his control sticks, checking his projected-targeting screen.

EXT. SURFACE OF THE DEATH STAR

Luke's ship barrels down the trench.

INT. DARTH VADER'S COCKPIT

Vader's targeting computer swings around into position. Vader takes careful aim on Luke's X-wing fighter.

VADER

I have you now.

He pushes the fire buttons.

EXT. SURFACE OF THE DEATH STAR

The three TIE fighters move in on Luke. As Vader's center fighter unleashes a volley of laserfire, one of the TIE ships at his side is hit and explodes into flame. The two remaining ships continue to move on.

INT. LUKE'S X-WING FIGHTER – COCKPIT

Luke looks about, wondering whose laserfire destroyed Vader's wingman.

INT. DARTH VADER'S COCKPIT

Vader is taken by surprise, and looks out from his cockpit.

> VADER
>
> What?

INT. DARTH VADER'S WINGMAN – COCKPIT

Vader's wingman searches around him, trying to locate the unknown attacker.

INT. *MILLENNIUM FALCON* – COCKPIT

Han and Chewbacca grin from ear to ear.

> HAN
> (yelling)
>
> Yahoo!

EXT. SPACE AROUND THE DEATH STAR

The Millennium Falcon *heads right at the two TIE fighters. It's a collision course.*

INT. WINGMAN'S COCKPIT

The wingman spots the pirateship coming at him and warns the Dark Lord.

> WINGMAN
>
> Look out!

EXT. DEATH STAR TRENCH

Vader's wingman panics at the sight of the oncoming pirate starship and veers radically to one side, colliding with Vader's TIE fighter in the process. Vader's wingman crashes into the side wall of the trench and explodes. Vader's ship spins out of the trench with a damaged wing.

EXT. SPACE AROUND THE DEATH STAR

Vader's ship spins out of control with a bent solar fin, heading for deep space.

INT. DARTH VADER'S COCKPIT

Vader turns round and round in circles as his ship spins into space.

EXT. SURFACE OF THE DEATH STAR

Solo's ship moves in towards the Death Star's trench.

INT. *MILLENNIUM FALCON* – COCKPIT

Solo, smiling, speaks to Luke over his headset mike.

> HAN
> *(into mike)*
> You're all clear, kid.

INT. MASSASSI OUTPOST – WAR ROOM

Leia and the others listen to Solo's transmission.

> HAN
> *(over speaker)*
> Now let's blow this thing and go home!

INT. LUKE'S X-WING FIGHTER – COCKPIT

Luke looks up and smiles. He concentrates on the exhaust port, then fires his laser torpedoes.

EXT. SURFACE OF THE DEATH STAR

Luke's torpedo shoots towards the port and seems simply to disappear into the surface and not explode. But the shots do find their mark and have gone into the exhaust port and are heading for the main reactor.

INT. LUKE'S X-WING FIGHTER – COCKPIT

Luke throws his head back in relief.

INT. DEATH STAR

An Imperial soldier runs to the control-panel board and pulls the attack lever as the board behind him lights up.

> VOICE
> (*over intercom*)

Stand by to fire at Rebel base.

EXT. SPACE AROUND THE DEATH STAR

Two X-wings, a Y-wing, and the pirateship race towards Yavin in the distance.

INT. DEATH STAR

Several Imperial soldiers, flanking a pensive Grand Moff Tarkin, busily push control levers and buttons.

> VOICE
> (*over intercom*)

Standing by.

The rumble of a distant explosion begins.

EXT. SPACE AROUND THE DEATH STAR

The Rebel ships race out of sight, leaving the moon like Death Star alone against a blanket of stars. Several small flashes appear on the surface. The Death Star bursts into a supernova, creating a spectacular heavenly display.

INT. *MILLENNIUM FALCON* – COCKPIT

> HAN

Great shot, kid. That was one in a million.

INT. LUKE'S X-WING FIGHTER – COCKPIT

Luke is at last at ease, and his eyes are closed.

> BEN'S VOICE

Remember, the Force will be with you . . . always.

The ship rocks back and forth.

EXT. DARTH VADER'S TIE FIGHTER

Vader's ship spins off into space.

EXT. SPACE

The Rebel ships race towards the fourth moon of Yavin.

INT. MASSASSI OUTPOST – MAIN HANGAR

Luke climbs out of his starship fighter and is cheered by a throng of ground crew and pilots. He climbs down the ladder as they all welcome him with laughter, cheers, and shouting.

Princess Leia rushes towards him.

> LEIA

Luke! Luke! Luke!

She throws her arms around Luke and hugs him as they dance around a circle. Solo runs in towards Luke and they embrace one another, slapping each other on the back.

> HAN
> (*laughing*)

Hey! Hey!

> LUKE
> (*laughing*)

I knew you'd come back! I just knew it!

> HAN

Well, I wasn't gonna let you get all the credit and take all the reward.

Luke and Han look at one another, as Solo playfully shoves at Luke's face. Leia moves in between them.

> LEIA
> (*laughing*)

Hey, I knew there was more to you than money.

Luke looks towards the ship.

> LUKE

Oh, no!

The fried little Artoo-Detoo is lifted off the back of the fighter and carried off under the worried eyes of Threepio.

THREEPIO

Oh, my! Artoo! Can you hear me? Say something!
(*to mechanic*)
You can repair him, can't you?

TECHNICIAN

We'll get to work on him right away.

THREEPIO

You must repair him! Sir, if any of my circuits or gears will
help, I'll gladly donate them.

LUKE

He'll be all right.

INT. MASSASSI OUTPOST – MAIN THRONE ROOM

*Luke, Han, and Chewbacca enter the huge ruins of the main temple.
Hundreds of troops are lined up in neat rows. Banners are flying and at
the far end stands a vision in white, the beautiful young Senator Leia.
Luke and the others solemnly march up the long aisle and kneel before
Senator Leia. From one side of the temple marches a shined-up and
fully repaired Artoo-Detoo. He waddles up to the group and stands next
to an equally pristine Threepio, who is rather awestruck by the whole
event. Chewbacca is confused. Dodonna and several other dignitaries sit
on the left of Princess Leia. Leia is dressed in a long white dress and is
staggeringly beautiful. She rises and places a gold medallion around
Han's neck. He winks at her. She then repeats the ceremony with Luke,
who is moved by the event. They turn and face the assembled troops,
who all bow before them. Chewbacca growls and Artoo beeps with
happiness.*

    FADE OUT. END CREDITS OVER STARS.